QUICK ESCAPES® FROM
New York City

· ·

The Best Weekend Getaways

EIGHTH EDITION

Susan Farewell

D1502879

travel

Guilford, Connecticut

All the information in this guidebook is subject to change.
We recommend that you call ahead to obtain current
information before traveling.

Editor: Amy Lyons
Project Editor: Lynn Zelem
Layout: Joanna Beyer
Text design: Sheryl Kober
Maps: M.A. Dubé, updated by Ryan Mitchell © Morris Book Publishing,
LLC

ISSN 1545-5726
ISBN 978-0-7627-5402-1

Printed in the United States of America
10 9 8 7 6 5 4 3 2 1

ABOUT THE AUTHOR

Susan Farewell first started exploring the areas around New York City as a child growing up in Salem, New York. Back then, she traveled with her family, notebook always in hand. She later went on to study at Boston University and then became a travel editor at the Condé Nast Publications in New York City and eventually left to write some of her own books and freelance articles.

She has written extensively about New England for many magazines and newspapers around the world and continues to travel throughout the region, year-round. Farewell says she never feels as though she has seen all of New England. "Every time I go, I discover new areas," she says. "Lakes I've never been to before, cross-country ski areas in dense wilderness, museums tucked away in places you wouldn't expect, art galleries, farms, factories, whole cities (!) and mile after mile of arrestingly beautiful scenery. . . . there's so much to explore."

In 2009, Susan launched an online travel magazine, *Farewell Travels: Select Escapes* (www.farewelltravels.com) which includes her travel recommendations to and at destinations around the world.

Farewell lives in Westport, Connecticut, with her author/ documentary filmmaker husband, Tom Seligson, and their daughter, Justine, her beloved traveling companions.

DEDICATION

For introducing me to travel and encouraging me to pursue my travel dreams, I dedicate this book, in loving memory, to my parents.

ACKNOWLEDGMENTS

I cannot just rattle off a half a dozen or so names of people who helped me with the research of this book. The list would go on and on for pages and include innkeepers, chefs, historians, curators, and tourism officials in all the states I covered. It would also include many of my colleagues and friends who are forever recommending places to visit and a large number of anonymous contributors whom I can only remember as "the blond boy on the bicycle in Nantucket" or "the couple on the ferry to Block Island."

Perhaps the two that deserve the most credit, however, are my husband, Tom Seligson, and our daughter, Justine. In order to do the constant research for this book (and its updates), they are forever enduring long car rides and hearing me say "Just one more stop, guys!" They are not only wonderful traveling buddies, but top-of-the-line research assistants as well. Tom has unflagging energy and curiosity and Justine (an observant traveler and writer herself) loves adventure. The two of them pick up on all sorts of details I may otherwise miss. I am so grateful to have them to explore the world with.

CONTENTS

INTRODUCTION

Have you ever gone away for the weekend without knowing precisely what places to visit (and the easiest way to get there), where to stay, and what to see and do once you have arrived? What should or could have been a little vacation can very often turn into a big disappointment. You find yourself saying things like "There must be some place we could just get a sandwich" or "Well, it cost only $5 to get in, not a major loss." Perhaps the most frequently uttered words of all, however, are "Next time." "Next time we'll stay at the inn on the water." "Next time we'll have brunch at that little restaurant in town." "Next time we'll leave enough time to hike to the summit." Unfortunately the "next time" may not happen very soon, if at all. It's hard enough finding the time to get away; the last thing you need is to have regrets.

It is precisely with those concerns in mind that I've compiled the twenty Quick Escapes that follow. They range in length from one to three nights and take you to some well-known and some hardly known destinations in New York State, New Jersey, Connecticut, Massachusetts, Rhode Island, and Vermont. For those of you who aren't traveling by car, I've included three trips you can make by using public transportation. Keep in mind, however, that several of the Quick Escapes can be done without a car.

Whether you're an out-of-towner visiting the New York area, a newcomer, or a longtime resident, this guide will help you find the places I've been lucky to have discovered or have had pointed out to me over the years as a child growing up in New York State, as a longtime resident of Connecticut, and as a travel writer.

Each escape is designed to be a little vacation in itself, offering you a combination platter of things to do and taking in the area's most noteworthy attractions. The itineraries are meant to be

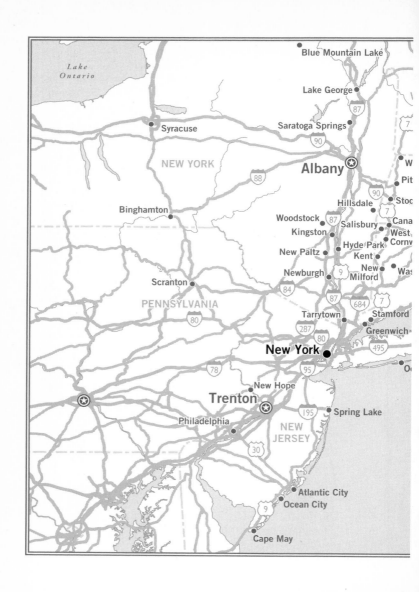

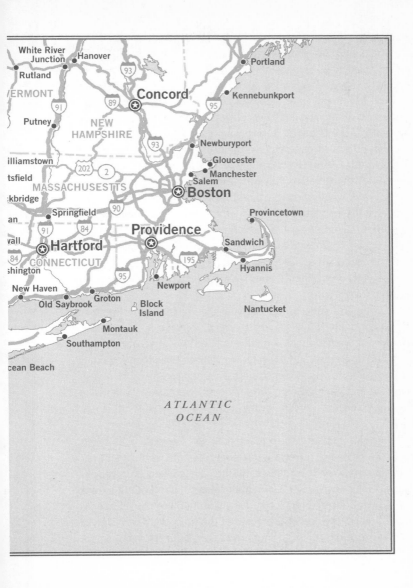

used as guides only, so feel free to improvise as you go along. If you see a road that looks compelling, by all means, follow it. Making your own discoveries can be lots of fun. You won't be able to fit in everything I suggest, so choose the things that most appeal to you and, if you have more time, consider combining trips.

In most of the locales, I've suggested restaurants (or great picnic spots) for all meals during your stay. In most cases there are several other eating places worthy of inclusion, some of which are listed under **Other Recommended Restaurants and Lodgings** at the end of the itinerary. Nevertheless there are still others, and to list them all would probably double the length of this book. For a complete list of restaurants and accommodations, contact the tourist offices listed under **For More Information** at the end of each escape.

In the resort areas, be sure to make restaurant reservations. Otherwise you can wait for hours. If it's a holiday weekend, reservations are a must.

I've avoided listing prices because they change so often and, in the case of hotels, can vary from season to season. The restaurants and accommodations I have included are generally moderately priced or on the splurgey side. My thinking was that you don't need this guide to locate the chain hotels and motels. The places I have selected generally are either full of character or otherwise special in some way, which, in many cases, translates into more money.

It's always a good idea to make lodging reservations as far in advance as possible, especially for shore destinations in summer and ski destinations in winter. Some inns are booked up a year in advance. Many of the island inns (and resort town inns) require a minimum two- or three-night stay for a summer weekend. For destinations all over the area, 99 percent of the time you'll be asked to give an advance deposit with your credit card or to send in a check to guarantee your room. Check-in time is generally between 2 and 3 in the afternoon; checkout is usually somewhere around noon.

Following each itinerary are lists of additional things to do in the area (from outlet shopping to horseback riding), special annual events, and contact numbers and addresses for more information.

To make your trip go as smoothly as possible, be prepared. Use the following as a checklist before setting out.

HANDY TAKE-ALONGS

Comfort on the road is important for you and your traveling companions. In addition to dressing comfortably, in loose-fitting layers, consider taking these items along:

- Water bottles that can be refilled along the way and/or a supply of nonalcoholic liquids
- Snacks (preferably dry or nonjuicy fruits, granola bars, crackers, raw veggies, trail mix)
- Pillow and blanket for passenger(s)
- Sunglasses
- Reading material for passenger(s)
- Good map or atlas and/or a GPS unit
- Umbrella
- Large box of tissues
- Pocket knife (with corkscrew)
- Camera
- Binoculars

For auto emergencies, be sure to have these items:

- A cell phone
- Phone card for pay phone calls
- Flares or reflector triangles

- Jumper cables
- Empty gas can
- Fire extinguisher
- Blanket
- Flashlight (and extra batteries)
- First-aid kit

If you're traveling with children:

- Crayons and coloring books
- Storybooks
- Games (remember that small pieces get lost easily)
- Wipes to clean up messes and sticky hands
- Any electronic devices your children like

If you're traveling with pets:

- Water dish and water supply
- Dry snacks
- Favorite toys
- Leash and/or pet carrier

If you're traveling in winter:

- Ice scraper
- Collapsible shovel
- Traction mats

SUGGESTED CLOTHING AND FOOTWEAR

What to pack for a trip outside New York City depends entirely on what time of year you go, since the weather varies so dramatically. Nevertheless, there are some items that may come in handy year-round. They include:

- A jacket and tie for men
- At least one dressy outfit for women
- Hiking boots
- A pair of sneakers or comfortable walking shoes
- A raincoat or poncho
- A robe (especially if you're staying at a bed-and-breakfast with the bathroom down the hall)
- A sweater (even in summer months)

And don't forget:

- Any prescriptions or medications
- A travel alarm
- Bug spray
- Sun protection (SPF lotion, hats)

GETTING IN AND OUT OF THE CITY

Getting caught in rush-hour traffic going out of or coming into Manhattan can put a real damper on a weekend getaway. Do yourself a huge favor and rearrange work schedules or any other responsibilities so you avoid heavy traffic completely. During the warm-weather months (especially in the height of summer), traffic heading out to Long Island, New Jersey, and virtually all points north and east of the city starts getting thick right around lunchtime on Fri afternoons. Same thing late Sun afternoon returning to the city. Otherwise, the customary rush hours (roughly 7 to 10 a.m. and 4 to 7 p.m.) should be avoided. Also, keep your eyes and ears open for events taking place. Something like the marathon or a presidential visit can keep you stalled in traffic for hours. A good radio station to tune into for these sorts of announcements is WINS (1010 on your AM dial).

NEW YORK *ESCAPES*

NEW YORK ESCAPE *One*
Hudson River Valley I
THE EAST BANK / 1 NIGHT

- River estates
- Farms
- Shaker Museum
- Historic houses
- Presidents' homes
- Firefighting museum
- Culinary Institute of America

As a major waterway, the **Hudson River,** which was first explored by Henry Hudson in 1609, is rich with history. Scattered along its banks there are historic riverfront towns and stately old mansions (built by the rich and famous) surrounded by thick woods and spectacular scenery.

You could easily make several trips to the Hudson Valley region and not retrace your steps. For this particular escape we take you north and east of the river through several rural towns and hamlets and then follow the river down along its eastern banks through some of the area's most historically interesting towns. This trip can be combined with the Hudson River Valley II and/or Hudson River Valley III escapes, which follow.

DAY 1 / MORNING

From Manhattan take the Henry Hudson Parkway north to the Saw Mill River Parkway to the Taconic State Parkway. At Route 44 turn east toward **Millbrook.** Home to many farms, Millbrook and the surrounding hamlets are well known among the horse enthusiasts. There are several worthwhile attractions in the Millbrook area, including **Wing's Castle** (717 Bangall Rd., off Route 44; 845-677-9085; www.wingscastle.com) built by artists Peter and Toni Wing. The castle, which is made from salvaged materials from antique

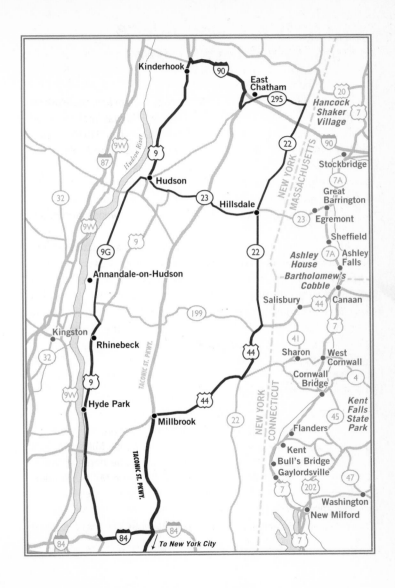

buildings, took them more than twenty-five years to complete. Tours are offered from the end of May through Christmas, Wed through Sun, 10 a.m. to 5 p.m. **The Institute of Ecosystem Studies Mary Flagler Cary Arboretum** (on the northern side of Route 44A, 1 mile from the junction with Route 44 to the west and 2 miles from the junction with Route 44 to the east; 845-677-5343; www.ecostud ies.org) is an ecological research and education center with nature trails, a perennial garden, a fern glen, a greenhouse, and a gift and plant shop. Hours vary seasonally, so call ahead. When you reach Route 22 at Millerton, take a left and head north. You'll soon reach **Taconic State Park** and **Copake Falls.** Follow the signs to Bash Bish Falls if you want to do a little hiking in a beautiful valley that has 50-foot falls as its centerpiece. From the parking lot it's about a mile-long (or twenty-minute) walk.

Afterward return to Route 22 and head north for a couple of miles until you reach Route 23. Turn right and follow signs for the **Catamount Ski Area** in Hillsdale (518-325-3200; www.cata mountski.com), where, come winter, there's snowboarding terrain as well as ski trails for all levels.

LUNCH The Swiss Hütte, adjacent to the ski area (Route 23, Hill-sdale, 518-325-3333; www.swisshutte.com), is a good lunch choice. It has every-thing from chef salad and burgers to filet of sole, plus a pretty view of Catamount Mountain, and is owned by a Swiss chef.

AFTERNOON

Continue north on Route 22 to Route 295 and turn left. Follow Route 295 for about 6 miles into East Chatham. Then go right on the Albany Turnpike for about 3 miles to **Old Chatham.** In Old Chatham turn left onto County Route 13 and follow that for about a mile. On the right you'll see the **Shaker Museum and Library,** 88 Shaker Museum Rd. (518-794-9100; www.shakermuseumand library.org), which showcases an unparalleled collection of Shaker furnishings in several farm buildings. The museum and library are open between late May and Oct from 10 a.m. to 5 p.m. Wed through Mon.

From Old Chatham it's a short drive to **Kinderhook** (follow Route 9H South), where you'll find three historic houses open to the public. The **James Vanderpoel House,** on Route 9 (518-758-9265), is a Federal mansion that was built around 1820. The **Luykas Van Alen House,** south of town on Route 9H (518-758-9265), was built in 1737 and is now a museum of 18th-century Dutch domestic culture. Both are maintained by the **Columbia County Historical Society** (www.cchsny.org) and are open Thurs through Sat from 11 a.m. to 5 p.m. and Sun from 1 to 5 p.m. from Memorial Day weekend through Labor Day weekend. A ticket bought at one house is good for visits to both of them.

Drive south another mile or so and you'll reach **Lindenwald,** which is also known as the **Martin Van Buren National Historic Site,** about 2 miles south of Kinderhook on Route 9H (518-758-9689; www.nps.gov/mava). This was the retirement home of the eighth president of the United States. The mansion and grounds are open daily for touring from 9 a.m. to 4:30 p.m. from late May through the end of Oct.

From Lindenwald continue south on Route 9H and then head east on Route 23 to Hillsdale, where you can settle in for the night and a memorable meal.

DINNER **Hillsdale House,** 1 Anthony St., Hillsdale (518-325-7111), has a wide selection of dishes (from pizza to steak au poivre) served at lunch and dinner, seven days a week. It's situated in an old historic inn that was built in 1813.

LODGING   Settle into the **Bell House Bed and Breakfast,** 9315 Route 22, Hillsdale (518-325-3841; www.bellhousebb.com), a five-room historic inn with a wraparound porch, beautiful old trees, and perennial gardens. Try to book the Edith Wharton Room, which overlooks the pool, lawns, and gardens. Its bathroom has an antique claw-foot tub.

DAY 2 / MORNING

BREAKFAST   A dreamy way to start the day, breakfast at the **Bell House Bed and Breakfast** is served on the front porch or the brick patio out back. Not for the calorie-conscious, it includes fresh fruit to start followed by baked goods and a main dish (eggs benedict, peaches-and-cream French toast).

Start by going west on Route 23 to the former whaling town of **Hudson.** Here you'll find several antiques shops as well as a fine collection of beautifully restored Federal, Greek Revival, and Victorian houses that were built in the 18th century. Detailed walking-tour maps are available in most of the shops. There's a firefighting museum in town, the **FASNY Museum of Firefighting,** 117 Harry Howard Ave. (518-822-1875; www.fasnyfiremuseum.com), which is filled with antique firefighting equipment including a 1725 fire engine. The museum is open daily year-round, from 9 a.m. to 4:30 p.m. except major holidays.

Head south of town on Route 9G and you'll come to **Olana State Historic Site,** about 5 miles south of Hudson (518-828-0135; www .olana.org). This was the home of the 19th-century landscape artist Frederic Edwin Church. He built Olana, a five-story Persian-style villa atop a bluff overlooking the Hudson, in the 1870s. There are forty-five-minute tours of the first floor from the beginning of Apr until the end of Dec. Tours run every half hour between 10 a.m. and 5 p.m.

Continue south on Route 9G and then west on Route 6 to **Clermont State Historic Site/Museum,** 1 Clermont Ave., Germantown (518-537-4240; www.friendsofclermont.org). Clermont was the home of Robert R. Livingston (and seven generations of his family), one of five men elected to draft the *Declaration of Independence.* He also was chancellor of New York and administered the oath of office to President George Washington. The house is open for touring (Apr through Oct, Tues through Sun 11 a.m. to 5 p.m., and Nov 1 through Mar 31, Sat and Sun 11 a.m. to 4 p.m.); the grounds are open year-round for hiking, riding, cross-country skiing, and picnicking.

A little farther south is **Rhinebeck,** which has a museum devoted to vintage airplanes, World War I aircraft, and other early craft. The **Old Rhinebeck Aerodrome,** off Route 9 at 42 Stone Church Rd. (845-752-3200; www.oldrhinebeck.org), is open from May 15 through Oct 31 daily from 10 a.m. to 5 p.m. Air shows are on Sat and Sun from mid-June through mid-Oct.

LUNCH   **Gigi Trattoria,** 6422 Montgomery St. (845-876-1007; www.gigitrattoria.com), serves gourmet pizzas, salads, paninis, and an array of pasta dishes.

AFTERNOON

After lunch spend a little time checking out the shops in Rhinebeck and then head south again on Route 9. In Staatsburg (between Rhinebeck and Hyde Park), take time out to see **Staatsburgh State Historic Site,** in Mills–Norrie State Park, off Route 9, Old Post Road (845-889-8851; www.staatsburgh.org). The Beaux Arts estate of Ogden and Ruth Livingston Mills is set on 900 acres. There are hiking trails, guided tours, and beautiful river views. It's open Tues through Sat from 10 a.m. to 4:30 p.m. and Sun from 11 a.m. to 4:30 p.m. Just before you reach **Hyde Park,** you'll come to the **Vanderbilt Mansion** (845-229-9115; www.nps.gov/vama). This fifty-four-room Beaux Arts mansion was designed by McKim, Mead & White for Frederick Vanderbilt. After a tour of the house, be sure to wander around the grounds. The view of the Hudson from here is nonpareil. The house is open 9 a.m. to 5 p.m. daily year-round; grounds are open daily from 7 a.m. until sunset.

Hyde Park, which is well known as the site of FDR's home, is next on the itinerary. You could easily spend an entire day (or more) here, especially if you're a history buff. Start with the **Home of Franklin D. Roosevelt National Historic Site,** 1 mile south of town on Route 9 (845-229-9115; www.nps.gov/hofr). This estate, known as Springwood, was the president's birthplace and lifelong residence. It's open daily 9 a.m. to 5 p.m. year-round; grounds are open daily from 7 a.m. until sunset. Adjacent is the **FDR Museum and Library,** which is filled with memorabilia, letters, documents, and photographs. It's open daily. Two miles east of the estate is the **Eleanor Roosevelt National Historic Site,** which is open daily from May through Oct and on Sat and Sun only from Nov through Apr. For information on all three places, call (845) 229-9115.

Once you've had your fill of presidential history, you can complete your journey with a wonderful meal at the Culinary Institute of America. Be sure to spend a bit of time poking around campus. Some of the world's greatest chefs got their start here.

DINNER   **The Culinary Institute of America,** Route 9 (845-471-6608; www.ciachef.edu). Be sure to call ahead for reservations at this highly esteemed cooking school. There are four student-staffed restaurants on the 150-acre campus: St. Andrew's Cafe offers contemporary dishes, the Caterina de Medici Dining Room features regional Italian cuisine, the Escoffier Room serves French cuisine, and the American Bounty Restaurant specializes in American food. The Apple Pie Bakery

Café showcases the talents of the school's baking and pastry arts students and faculty.

It's about a ninety-minute trip back to New York City from here. Take Route 9 south to I-84 east and then pick up the Taconic State Parkway heading south.

There's More . . . .

Architectural Wonders. **The Richard B. Fisher Center** for the Performing Arts at Bard College (Annandale-on-Hudson; 845-758-7950; www.bard.edu/fishercenter/) is a must see. It was designed by Frank Gehry, who is most well known for the Guggenheim Museum in Bilbao, Spain. Tours of the glass, concrete, and stainless-steel 110,000-square-foot building are offered daily at 11 a.m., 1 p.m., and 2 p.m.

Hiking. **Poet's Walk,** County Road 103, north of the Rhinecliff–Kingston Bridge, Red Hook; (845) 473-4440; www.scenichudson.org. A 120-acre park with trails for hiking and benches scattered about.

Historic Houses. **Montgomery Place,** River Road, Annandale-on-Hudson; (845) 758-5461. This 19th-century estate is set on hundreds of acres overlooking the Hudson River and the Catskill Mountains. There are gardens, a greenhouse, nature trails, and pick-your-own-fruit orchards.

Vineyards. **Cascade Mountain Winery,** 835 Cascade Mountain Rd., Amenia; (845) 373-9021; www.cascademt.com. Tours and tastings offered. There's also a cafe and picnic area. Open year-round, Thurs through Sun, 11 a.m. to 5 p.m. Lunch is served between noon and 3 p.m. and dinner on Sat nights.

Millbrook Vineyards and Winery, Wing Road and Shunpike Road, Millbrook; (845) 677-8383; www.millbrookwine.com. Tours and tastings. Open year-round daily from noon to 5 p.m. (11 a.m. to 6 p.m. summer months).

Special Events . . . .

MAY, JULY, OCTOBER
Rhinebeck Antiques Fair. Dealers from all over New England show furniture, folk art, paintings, etc. At the Dutchess County Fairgrounds, Rhinebeck; (845) 876-1989; www.rhinebeckantiquesfair.com.

JUNE
Crafts at Rhinebeck. A juried show of more than 350 exhibitors. Held at the Dutchess County Fairgrounds, Rhinebeck; (845) 876-4001; www.dutchessfair.com.

AUGUST
Annual Shaker Museum Antiques Festival, Shaker Museum, Old Chatham; (518) 794-9100; www.shakermuseumandlibrary.org. More than one hundred dealers.

SEPTEMBER
Annual Radio Control Jamboree. An air show and other aerial events at the Old Rhinebeck Aerodrome, Rhinebeck; (845) 752-3200; www.oldrhinebeck.org.

OCTOBER
Crafts at Rhinebeck Fall Festival. More than 200 exhibitors plus harvest-related activities. At the Dutchess County Fairgrounds, Rhinebeck; (845) 876-4001; www.dutchessfair.com.

Other Recommended Restaurants and Lodgings. . . .

AMENIA
Cascade Mountain Winery and Restaurant, 835 Cascade Mountain Rd.; (845) 373-9021; www.cascademt.com. Thurs through Sun, lovely lunches made with ultrafresh ingredients are served. Dinner is served on Sat nights.

Troutbeck, Leedsville Rd.; (845) 373-9681; www.troutbeck.com. This 1920s-era stone manor house on a Dutchess County estate has a split personality. During the week it's an executive retreat for conferences, and on weekends it's a romantic country inn. Troutbeck is exquisitely furnished with antiques throughout. Its dining room is a great find, serving contemporary American cuisine.

DOVER PLAINS
Old Drovers Inn, Old Post Rd. (Route 22 near Millbrook); (845) 832-9311; www.olddroversinn.com. This old inn (it's been welcoming visitors for more than 250 years) is a member of the elite Relais & Châteaux hotel group. It's full of old-fashioned charm and has a respectable restaurant specializing in innovative American cuisine. There are only four guest suites, so be sure to make reservations in advance.

MILLBROOK
Café les Baux, 152 Church St.; (845) 677-8166; www.cafelesbaux .com. A great choice for lunch, you'll find a selection of salads and sandwiches as well as more substantial entrees, including deliriously good fish dishes by owner Herve Bochard, a classical French chef.

RHINEBECK

Belvedere Mansion, 10 Old Route 9; (845) 889-8000; www.bel vederemansion.com. This is both a bed-and-breakfast and a restaurant that serves exquisite French American cuisine made from many local products. Many of its cooks and wait staff are alumni and students of the Culinary Institute.

Foster's Coach House, 9193 Montgomery St. (Route 9); (845) 876-8052; www.fosterscoachhouse.com. If you're in the mood for a burger, a sandwich, or something else simple and American, you can't go wrong with Foster's.

For More Information . . . .

Columbia County Office of Tourism, 401 State St., Hudson, NY 12534; (518) 828-3375 or (800) 724-1846; www.columbia countyny.org.

Dutchess County Tourism Promotion Agency, 3 Neptune Rd., Poughkeepsie, NY 12601; (845) 463-4000 or (800) 445-3131; www.dutchesstourism.com.

Historic Hudson Valley, 150 White Plains Rd., Tarrytown, NY 10591; (914) 631-8200; www.hudsonvalley.org.

Hudson Valley Tourism, P.O. Box 2840, Salt Point, NY 12578; (800) 232-4782; www.travelhudsonvalley.org.

New York State Division of Tourism, 30 Pearl St., Albany, NY 12245; (518) 474-4116 or (800) 225-5697; www.iloveny.com.

NEW YORK ESCAPE *Two*
Hudson River Valley II
THE LOWER HUDSON / 1 NIGHT

Both the east and west banks of the Lower Hudson are liberally sprinkled with historic, contemporary, and natural attractions. To take in the highlights of the area, we suggest driving up the eastern shore, crossing over on I-84, and

- Riverside towns and scenery
- Historic houses and estates
- Wonderful restaurants
- Museums
- Washington's Headquarters

then returning on the western banks. This trip can be combined with Hudson River Valley I escape and/or Hudson River Valley III escape.

DAY 1 / MORNING

Head north out of New York City on the Henry Hudson Parkway to the Saw Mill River Parkway. Then jog over to Route 9 in Hastings, an exit off the Saw Mill River Parkway. Route 9 roughly follows the Hudson shoreline, taking you through a string of historic towns and attractions.

Make your first destination **Tarrytown,** a riverside town that was settled by the Dutch in the mid-1600s and later made famous by the writings of Washington Irving, particularly The Legend of Sleepy Hollow. There are several noteworthy attractions in the area, including **Lyndhurst,** 635 South Broadway (914-631-4481; www .lyndhurst.org), a Gothic Revival estate that was the former home of financier Jay Gould. It's open for touring Tues through Sun from 10 a.m. to 5 p.m. between mid-Apr and Oct and on Sat and Sun only from Nov through mid-Apr. You can visit Irving's Hudson River

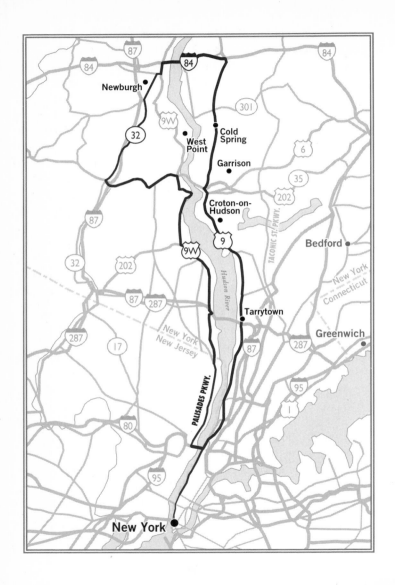

estate **Sunnyside,** on West Sunnyside Lane (914-591-8763; www
.hudsonvalley.org), which is open Wed through Mon between Apr
and Dec from 10 a.m. to 5 p.m. This estate, along with several other
properties that follow, is under the care of Historic Hudson Valley,
a nonprofit organization, which will gladly provide you with more
information (see address and telephone number under "For More
Information"). In nearby North Tarrytown you'll find **Philipsburg
Manor,** on Route 9, Sleepy Hollow (914-631-8200; www.hudson
valley.org), a beautifully restored 17th-century manor house with
a mill and millpond. It's also open daily year-round. Also in North
Tarrytown is **Kykuit** (pronounced "kye-kit."), a Rockefeller estate in
Sleepy Hollow, accessible by shuttle bus from Philipsburg Manor
(914-631-9491; www.hudsonvalley.org), which is open for public
viewing. It's a forty-room colonial revival mansion, on eighty-seven
lush acres, dotted with sculpture by modern masters including
Alexander Calder, Henry Moore, and Lois Nevelson. Nearby you'll
find **Union Church of Pocantico Hills** (for directions, visit www.hudson
valley.org), with stained-glass windows by Marc Chagall and Henri
Matisse. It was commissioned by members of the Rockefeller family; tours are offered from Apr through Dec.

Continue up Route 9 to **Van Cortlandt Manor,** in **Croton-on-
Hudson** (914-271-8981; www.hudsonvalley.org), which is a
restored baronial manor offering insight into the life of a wealthy
family in the early 1800s.

From there carry on to **Garrison,** which is home to **Boscobel**
(Route 9D; 845-265-3638; www.boscobel.org), an early-18th-
century country home open for touring. It's an acclaimed example
of Federal architecture. There are guided tours indoors and gar-
dened grounds outside overlooking the Hudson River.

Just to the north is the village of **Cold Spring,** where you can
settle in for a wonderful lunch, a relaxing afternoon, and the night.
The town is filled with historic 19th-century buildings.

LUNCH   **Plumbush Inn,** 1656 Route 9D (845-265-3904; www.plum bushinn.net), is a beautiful Victorian restaurant on five woodland acres. Lunch is a bit of a splurge, but worth it. The cuisine is largely continental. Lunch and dinner are served seven days a week.

AFTERNOON

Spend the afternoon poking around the many antiques and crafts shops in Cold Spring and check out the Putnam County Historical Society and **Foundry School Museum,** 63 Chestnut St. (845-265-4010; www.pchs-fsm.org), which displays Hudson River School paintings. The museum is open Mar through Dec, Tues and Wed from 10 a.m. to 4 p.m., Thurs from 1 to 4 p.m., and Sun from 2 to 5 p.m.

DINNER   **Cathryn's Tuscan Grill,** 91 Main St. (845-265-5582; www .tuscangrill.com), serves Tuscan-inspired cuisine. It has the kind of menu that keeps you saying to the wait person, "Please give us one more minute to choose," because there are so many wonderful options.

LODGING   **Hudson House,** 2 Main St. (845-265-9355; www.hudson houseinn.com), is an attractive twelve-room country inn on the banks of the Hudson River.

DAY 2 / MORNING

BREAKFAST   On Sat and Sun mornings, a full breakfast is included in the room price at **Hudson House.** During the week a continental breakfast is served.

After breakfast drive north via Route 301 from Cold Spring to Route 9 north and then take I-84 west over the river and head into

Newburgh to see **Washington's Headquarters State Historic Site,** Liberty and Washington Streets (84 Liberty St.; 845-562-1195; www.nysparks.com). From here Washington commanded his troops from 1781 to 1782. The headquarters are open between Apr and Oct, Wed through Sat from 10 a.m. to 5 p.m. and Sun from 1 to 5 p.m.

From Newburgh head south on Route 32 about 7 miles or so until you see a sign for the **Storm King Art Center,** 1 Pleasant Hill Rd., Mountainville (845-534-3115; www.stormking.org). Plan to spend several hours here: Storm King is the leading outdoor sculpture park and museum in the United States. It sprawls over 400 acres of lawns, terraces, fields, and woods. Visiting hours are from 11 a.m. to 5:30 p.m. daily from Apr 1 through late Oct and 11 a.m. to 5 p.m. from late Oct through Nov 15.

Continue south to **West Point,** home of the **United States Military Academy.** Founded in 1802, this spectacularly situated academy (it crowns a bluff high above the Hudson) has turned out many prominent leaders including Robert E. Lee, Ulysses S. Grant, and George S. Patton. The best time to visit is during spring or fall when the cadets parade or a sporting event takes place. There's a museum devoted to military history. The visitor center is located at 2107 New South Post Rd.; (845) 938-2638; www.usma.edu. The visitor center is open daily (with the exception of Thanksgiving, Christmas, and New Year's Day), from 9 a.m. to 4:45 p.m.

LUNCH The Thayer Hotel (674 Thayer Rd.; 845-446-4731 or 800-247-5047; www.thethayerhotel.com) inside West Point has a great lunch buffet daily and brunch on Sun. During the summer months, there's alfresco dining with far-reaching views of the Hudson River and Constitution Island. The hotel was built in 1926 and is listed on the National Register of Historic Places.

AFTERNOON

From West Point take Route 9W South and get off at the Haver-straw exit to reach **Bear Mountain State Park** (845-786-2701; www .hudsonriver.com), a 5,067-acre park that extends westward from the Hudson. Here you'll find an excellent **Trailside Museum,** which consists of several small museums, including a reptile museum, a nature-study museum, a geology museum, and a history museum. There are also hiking trails, picnic areas, a mountaintop observatory, and a breathtakingly beautiful drive up the mountain called **Perkins Memorial Drive.**

Once you've soaked up the serenity of the park, you can head back into Manhattan (which is a mere 45 miles away), taking the dramatically scenic Palisades Parkway south to the George Washington Bridge.

There's More . . . .

Hiking. **Hudson Highland State Park,** just north of Cold Spring, has lots of trails to wander along, as does the **Manitoga Nature Preserve,** south of Garrison. In nearby Carmel the Appalachian Trail cuts right through **Clarence Fahnestock State Park.** Visit www.nysparks.state .ny.us for more information.

Clarence Fahnestock State Park is off the Taconic State Parkway on Route 301 in Cold Spring. Extra-challenging is Breakneck Ridge, a hike just north of Cold Spring. The first half mile is straight up (though it's not really rock climbing, you do have to use your hands sometimes to hold onto rocks), but it's well worth it. The views—up and down the Hudson and inland a bit—are astonishingly beautiful. If you have time (you'll need a total of two or three hours), do the entire loop trip. You'll sleep well afterward. Also check out **Croton Point Park,** off Route 9 in Croton-on-Hudson.

Hudson River History. The **Hudson River Museum,** 511 Warburton Ave. in nearby Yonkers; (914) 963-4550; www.hrm.org. This museum includes Glenview Mansion, a Hudson River house overlooking the Palisades; a planetarium; and regional art, history, and science exhibits.

Kayaking. You can rent kayaks or go out for guided kayak tours through **Hudson Valley Outfitters,** 63 Main St., Cold Spring (845-265-0221 or 866-TO-KAYAK; www.hudsonvalleyoutfitters.com).

Skiing and other winter sports. For cross-country skiing, head to **Fahnestock Winter Park** in Cold Spring (75 Mountain Laurel Lane; 845-225-3998). This Hudson Valley park tends to have better snow than other local areas because it has a higher elevation—1,100 feet. It also has a very woodsy trail system and it maintains a great base, which is groomed for both classic and ski skating. There's always a wood-burning fire outside, around which red-cheeked skiers congregate to warm their hands and feet. There are also snowshoe trails and a hill for sledding and tubing.

Special Events . . . .

OCTOBER

Autumn Crafts & Tasks Festival, Van Cortlandt Manor, Croton. Demonstrations of house and farm labor in the 1700s, www.hudson valley.org.

Annual Arts and Crafts Festival, Bear Mountain State Park. A juried indoor and outdoor show.

DECEMBER

Candlelight Tours at Sunnyside, Philipsburg Manor, and Van Cortlandt Manor. English Christmas celebration, www.hudsonvalley.org.

Other Recommended Restaurants and Lodgings . . . .

BEAR MOUNTAIN

Bear Mountain Inn, Bear Mountain State Park; (845) 786-2731; www.visitbearmountain.com. Built in 1915, this rustic, sixty-room hunting lodge has its charms. You can stay overnight or grab a simple meal.

COLD SPRING

Pig Hill Inn, 73 Main St.; (845) 265-9247; www.pighillinn.com. The antiques throughout this three-story inn can be purchased. There are nine guest rooms, five with private baths. Pssst . . . the breakfasts alone make it worth staying here.

CROTON-ON-HUDSON

Alexander Hamilton House, 49 Van Wyck St.; (914) 271-6737; www.alexanderhamiltonhouse.com. Propped up on a cliff overlooking the Hudson River, this eight-room inn is a special find. All rooms have private baths, some have fireplaces, and two have two-person whirlpool baths.

For More Information . . . .

Dutchess County Tourism, 3 Neptune Rd., Poughkeepsie, NY 12601; (845) 463-4000; www.dutchesstourism.com.

Historic Hudson Valley, 150 White Plains Rd., Tarrytown, NY 10591; (914) 631-8200; www.hudsonvalley.org.

Hudson Valley Tourism, P.O. Box 2840, Salt Point, NY 12578; (800) 232-4782; www.travelhudsonvalley.org.

New York State Division of Tourism, 30 Pearl St., Albany, NY 12245; (518) 474-4116 or (800) 225-5697; www.iloveny.com.

Orange County Tourism, 20 Matthews St., Suite 111, Goshen, NY 10924; (800) 762-8687; www.orangetourism.org.

Putnam County Visitors Bureau, 110 Old Route 6, Carmel, NY 10512; (845) 225-0381 or (800) 470-4854; www.visitputnam .org.

NEW YORK ESCAPE *Three*

Hudson River Valley III
THE WEST BANK / 2 NIGHTS

- Mountain scenery
- Sports resorts
- Wineries
- Farms
- Maritime history
- Skiing

Back in 1820, author and historian Washington Irving wrote the tale of Rip Van Winkle, in which Rip joins a party of gnomes in the Catskill Mountains and falls asleep for twenty years. These modest but magical mountains, which can have a calming effect on anyone who visits them, can be reached in less than two hours from Manhattan.

Though the real magnet of the area is **Catskill Park,** which covers 705,500 acres, there are several river towns just to the east and south that are not only gateways to the park but attractions in themselves.

For this trip we suggest you start just south of the park, exploring the countryside around New Paltz, then head north to **Kingston,** which, back in 1777, was New York State's first capital. From there we take you into the Catskill Forest, to **Shandaken** in the mountains and Woodstock, which is the Catskills' most famous town.

DAY 1 / MORNING

Take the Henry Hudson Parkway up to the George Washington Bridge and cross over to the Palisades Interstate Parkway. Take that to the New York State Thruway north up to exit 18, which is **New Paltz.**

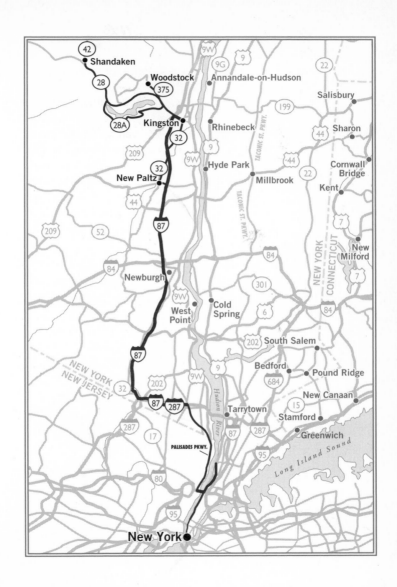

Head right for the Mohonk Mountain House, a National Historic Landmark and your home for the night, where you'll have a chance to wander about its wooded trails and feast your eyes on the lake for which the resort is named (mohonk means "lake in the sky"). For the best view of all, climb the cliff-top observation tower.

LUNCH Mohonk Mountain House, 1000 Mountain Rest Rd. (845-255-1000; www.mohonk.com), has a hot and cold buffet for lunch (included in the room rate).

AFTERNOON

Spend the afternoon visiting the wineries and other attractions along the **Shawangunk Wine Trail** (www.shawangunkwinetrail.com), a 30-mile loop (well marked with signs) that encompasses several Ulster County wineries, including Applewood Winery, 82 Four Corners Rd., Warwick (845-988-9292); Adair Vineyards, 52 Allhusen Rd. (845-255-1377), and many others. Bear in mind that you could make an entire day out of this, so the sooner you head out after lunch, the better. Visiting hours vary from vineyard to vineyard, but generally the vineyards are open during summer months until 5 p.m. Maps are available at the individual vineyards and tourism offices.

DINNER Mohonk Mountain House, 1000 Mountain Rest Rd. (845-255-1000; www.mohonk.com). Dinners in the dining room (included in the room rate) are usually traditional American dishes, though there are often other choices featured as daily specials.

LODGING Mohonk Mountain House is a big old-fashioned country hotel surrounded by the arrestingly beautiful scenery of the Shawangunk Mountains (right next to the Catskill Mountains). There's golf, tennis, hiking, and horseback riding—you name it.

DAY 2 / MORNING

BREAKFAST   Start the day with a big traditional American breakfast (included in the room rate) at **Mohonk House.**

After breakfast head into town to see **Huguenot Street,** which is the oldest street in the United States where original buildings still stand. New Paltz was founded back in 1678 by half a dozen Huguenots who were granted land by the colonial governor of New York. Huguenot Street is lined with several stone houses and a church, which were built between 1692 and 1799. All are open to the public for guided tours only from May 1 through Oct 31. Contact the **Huguenot Historical Society** (18 Broadhead Ave.; 845-255-1660; www.hhs-newpaltz.org) for more information.

From New Paltz head north on Route 32 toward Kingston. Along the way consider stopping in at **Apple Hill Farm,** 141 Route 32 South (845-255-0917; www.applehillfarm.com), where you can pick your own apples and pumpkins during the fall season.

Kingston is an old river port that was founded in 1652 as a Dutch trading settlement and became New York State's first capital in 1777. Many of its early buildings still stand today and are open to the public, including the **Old Dutch Church,** 272 Wall St. (845-338-6759), and the **Senate House,** 312 Fair St. (845-338-2786). All tour sites are either in or adjacent to the historic district, which is known as the Stockade because of the walls that used to surround it. Other Kingston attractions include the **Hudson River Maritime Museum and Rondout Lighthouse,** One Rondout Landing (845-338-0071; www.ulster.net/~hrmm), which is devoted to the maritime history of the area (open Fri through Mon 11 a.m. to 4 p.m.), and the **Trolley Museum of New York,** 89 East Strand (845-331-3399; www .tmny.org), which showcases old trolley cars. The Trolley Museum is open between Memorial Day and Columbus Day on Sat, Sun, and holidays from noon to 5 p.m. Also worthwhile is the **Volunteer Firemen's Hall and Museum of Kingston,** 265 Fair St. (845-331-0866). Open Fri 11 a.m. to 3 p.m. and Sat 10 a.m. to 4 p.m., summer only.

LUNCH   **Le Canard Enchaine,** (276 Fair St.; 845-339-2003; www .le-canardenchainesrestaurant.com) has a nice selection of healthy sandwiches as well as a selection of French entrees that vary daily.

AFTERNOON

Once you've had a look around Kingston, head west on Route 28, which runs through the **Catskill Park and Forest Preserve,** a large part of the Catskills under the protection of the government. A great place to hike is the **Slide Mountain Wilderness Area,** which is home to **Slide Mountain,** the highest peak in the Catskills.

Slide Mountain Wilderness Area encompasses over 47,500 acres. A list of trail access points can be found on the Web site www.dec.state.ny.us (search: Slide Mountain).

DINNER   **Catskill Rose,** Route 212, Mount Tremper (845-688-7100; www.catskillrose.com), prides itself on its variety of American and European dishes. Serves dinner only.

LODGING   **The Copperhood Inn and Spa,** Route 28, Shandaken (845-688-2460; www.copperhood.com) is an eighteen-room inn with a spa as well as a 60-foot indoor swimming pool. It's located between Phoenicia and Shandaken on Route 28.

DAY 3 / MORNING

After breakfast at the **Copperhead Inn** (and perhaps a spa treatment or two), head back onto Route 28, detouring on Route 28A for some more beautiful scenery around the 12-milelong Asholkan reservoir, and then follow Route 375 into **Woodstock.** Here you can spend hours browsing through shops and galleries before heading back to New York City. Don't miss the **Woodstock Artists Association Gallery,** 28 Tinker St. at Village Green (845-679-2940; www .woodstockart.org). It has been the center of the community since 1920, featuring works by both local and nationally known artists.

LUNCH Joshua's, 51 Tinker St. (845-679-5533; www.joshuascafe .com), is right in town and offers a good selection of sandwiches and vegetarian dishes, plus some Middle Eastern dishes as well.

From Woodstock it's a short drive east to I-87, which you take south back to the New York metropolitan area.

There's More . . . .

Biking. Mountain and road bikes can be rented at **Bicycle Depot,** 15 Main St., New Paltz (845-255-3859; www.bicycledepot.com) and at **Overlook Mountain Bikes,** 93 Tinker St., Woodstock (845-679-2122; www.overlookmountainbikes.com).

Bird-watching. **Slide Mountain** is an especially good place for bird-watching. Among its many inhabitants are wild turkeys, ruffed grouse, pileated woodpeckers, yellow-bellied sapsuckers, and several different warblers and thrushes.

Golf. **Mohonk Mountain House** in New Paltz (845-255-1000), and **Green Acres Golf Club** in Kingston (845-331-2283).

Hudson River boat tours. In Kingston several boat companies offer river trips. Among them are **Hudson River Cruises** (845-340-4700; www.hudsonrivercruises.com), which has music and dinner cruises, **North River Cruises** (845-679-8205; www.northrivercruises.com), and the **Great Hudson Sailing Center** (845-429-1557; www.great hudsonsailing.com), which offers sailing trips.

Parks and preserves. **Cohotate Preserve,** Greene County Environmental Education Center, Route 385, north of the Rip Van Winkle Bridge, near Athens; (518) 622-3620.

    Four Mile Point Preserve, Route 385, Four Mile Point Road, near Coxsackie; (845) 473-4440; www.scenichudson.org.

    Ramshorn–Livingston Sanctuary, off Route 9W, Grandview Avenue, Catskill; (845) 473-4440; www.scenichudson.org. A tidal swamp with more than 480 acres operated by the North Catskills Audubon Society.

Skiing. For downhill skiing, there's **Hunter Mountain** in Hunter (800-486-8376; www.huntermtn.com); **Belleayre Mountain** in Highmount (845-254-5600; www.belleayre.com); **Ski Windham** in Windham (800-754-9463; www.windhammountain.com); and **Ski Plattekill** near Roxbury (607-326-3500; www.plattekill.com). For cross-country skiing, there's **Mountain Trails Cross-Country Center** in Tannersville (518-589-5361; www.mttrails.com) and **Belleayre Mountain** in Highmount (845-254-5600; www.belleayre.com).

Special Events . . . .

AUGUST

Ulster County Fair, an annual event at the Fairgrounds, 2 miles southwest of New Paltz on Libertyville Road.

SEPTEMBER

Hudson Valley Food Festival, uptown Kingston, Wall Street area. Includes music, tastings, and demonstrations.

Hudson Valley Garlic Festival, Cantine Field (exit 20 off the Governor Thomas E. Dewey Thruway), Saugerties. Food, cooking demonstrations, lectures, crafts, and entertainment.

Harvest Moon Festival at the Hudson River Maritime Museum, Rondout Landing, Kingston. Seasonal foods, music, exhibits.

Other Recommended Restaurants and Lodgings . . . .

HIGH FALLS

Depuy Canal House, Route 213; (845) 687-7700; www.depuy canalhouse.net. This very special restaurant is in a landmark historic stone building that used to be a tavern (back in 1797). The menu—some seafood, some meat dishes—changes frequently.

HIGHLAND

Rocking Horse Ranch Resort, 600 Route 44–45; (845) 691-2927; www.rhranch.com. A great choice for families, this resort is a dude ranch complete with horseback riding, all-you-can-eat chuck-wagon cuisine, and a whole "alphabet of activities."

NEW PALTZ

Locust Tree Inn, 215 Huguenot St.; (845) 255-7888; www.locust tree.com. An attractive restaurant serving chicken, lamb, and fish dishes. It overlooks a golf course.

SAUGERTIES

Saugerties Lighthouse, P.O. Box 654, Saugerties 12477; (845) 247-0656; www.saugertieslighthouse.com. A truly unique experience, visitors can stay in this historic two-bedroom lighthouse. The rooms fill quickly, especially weekends in the fall, so be sure to book well in advance.

For More Information . . . .

Historic Hudson Valley, 150 White Plains Rd., Tarrytown, NY 10591; (914) 631-8200; www.hudsonvalley.org.

Hudson Valley Tourism, P.O. Box 2840, Salt Point, NY 12578; (800) 232-4782; www.travelhudsonvalley.org.

New Paltz Chamber of Commerce, 124 Main St., New Paltz, NY 12561; (845) 255-0243; www.newpaltzchamber.org.

New York State Division of Tourism, 30 Pearl St., Albany, NY 12245; (518) 474-4116 or (800) 225-5697; www.iloveny.com.

Ulster County Public Information, 10 Westbrook Lane, Kingston, NY 12401; (800) 342-5826; www.co.ulster.ny.us.

Woodstock Chamber of Commerce, P.O. Box 36, Woodstock, NY 12498; (845) 679-6234; www.woodstockchamber.com.

NEW YORK ESCAPE *Four*
Northern Westchester County
HORSE COUNTRY / 2 NIGHTS

If you thought you had to drive for five or six (well, at least three) hours to get to someplace that's very New England, you'll be pleasantly surprised to discover this little chunk of the world.

Galleries and museums
Concerts
Rural countryside
Colonial houses
Antiques shops
Fine dining
Horse farms
Hiking

Just a little over an hour's drive from Manhattan, there are at least half a dozen little towns or hamlets (including Bedford, Katonah, North and South Salem, and Pound Ridge) that could easily pass for New England. They're small, they're home to antiques shops, galleries, and little bistros selling fragrant soups on chilly days, and they're surrounded by woods and streams and lakes that really do sparkle. Drive down Main Street in South Salem on an autumn day, and yes, you will think you took a wrong turn somewhere and ended up in New Hampshire.

This little corner of southeastern New York, right on the border of Connecticut, is not only scenic but also very culturally active. There are several museums and galleries, music festivals, and some restaurants that, on their own, warrant a trip to the area. On top of that, however, there are some diversions you can find only in rural areas, including pick-your-own orchards, horse shows at sprawling farms, and hundreds of acres of woodland preserved for public use.

Unfortunately, there are really no places to stay, aside from a Holiday Inn in nearby Mount Kisco. Nevertheless, Ridgefield, Connecticut, which is home to a couple of country inns, is just over the border from both North and South Salem, and New Canaan,

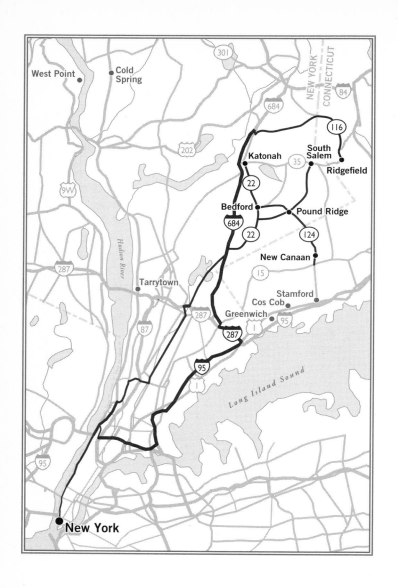

Connecticut, is just beyond Pound Ridge, New York. You can very easily combine this trip with our Ridgefield and New Canaan escape.

DAY 1 / MORNING

To reach the area, head north on either I-684 or the Saw Mill River Parkway. Both will get you to the Bedford/Katonah exits in just about an hour's time. In fact the Saw Mill River Parkway merges with I-684, where you should exit (exit 6, Katonah/Cross River). Turn right onto Route 35, take it to the first stoplight, and then turn right onto Route 22. About half a mile or so up on the left, you'll see the signs for the **Katonah Museum of Art,** Route 22 East at Jay Street (914-232-9555; www.katonah-museum.org), your first stop of the day.

Firmly ensconced in local history, this museum, which originally occupied a small room in the Katonah Village Library, showcases between eight and ten exhibitions a year from a variety of periods, cultures, and mediums, many of which have received national recognition. There's also a sculpture garden. Open Tues through Sat from 10 a.m. to 5 p.m., and Sun from noon to 5 p.m.

Right across from the museum, you'll see Jay Street, which takes you into the town of **Katonah,** where you can pause for lunch and a look around some artsy shops.

LUNCH **Willy Nick's Café,** 17 Katonah Ave. (914-232-8030; www .willynicks.com), serves creative New American dishes plus burgers, salads, and pizzas. There are tables outside for eating alfresco when the weather's good.

AFTERNOON

From town retrace your steps on Jay Street back to Route 22, where you'll turn right. Follow Route 22 for a little more than a mile and you'll see the **John Jay Homestead State Historic Site,** 400 Route 22 (914-232-5651; www.johnjayhomestead.org), on the left. This large farmhouse, built in 1787, housed the Jay family up until the 1960s. Costumed hostesses take visitors around, pointing out the furnishings that belonged to John Jay and the family generations that followed. Hours and dates the house is open change through the year, so it's best to call ahead. If you're visiting during the year-end holidays, there are scheduled holiday house tours and marionette shows for both children and adults.

Just beyond the homestead, turn left onto Girdle Ridge Road at the concrete dividers. About half a mile down on the right is the **Caramoor Center for Music and the Arts** (914-232-5035; www .caramoor.org), which contains both a house museum and a Venetian theater surrounded by formal gardens. The house, a Mediterranean-style villa painted pink, was originally the country home of Walter Tower Rosen, a lawyer and investment banker. It's filled with artwork and antiques that he and his wife collected from palaces throughout Europe. Entire rooms, in fact, were brought over, including a library from a French château and a pine-paneled room from a home in England. Performances, which include those by concert pianists, chamber groups, and opera companies, are held during the summer months. For a schedule and programs and to order tickets, visit their Web site. The house is open for touring Wed through Sun from 1 to 4 p.m. from May through Oct and between Nov and Apr by appointment only.

One of Bedford's most scenic roads, **Hook Road,** is right behind Caramoor. Well worn by the hooves of horses, the dirt route takes you past big old houses surrounded by woods and gardens and through countryside that feels a million miles away from the concrete chasms of New York City.

Follow Hook Road to the end and you'll be back on Route 22 (called Cantitoe Street here). Turn left and it'll take you right into

Bedford Village, a treasure box of a town with impeccably cared for colonial houses, historic buildings, and a flawless green. Bedford Village was settled back in 1680 and became a popular country retreat for wealthy families in the mid-1800s. Many of the buildings were built after the Revolution (since most were burned by the British in 1779) and are lovingly preserved by the Bedford Historical Society. These include the 1787 Court House (the oldest public building in Westchester County) and the one-room schoolhouse, which are open for touring from May to Oct. Other historic buildings and sites include the old burial ground, the general store (1838), and the Bedford Free Library (1807). Contact the Bedford Historical Society (914-234-9751; www.bedfordhistoricalsociety.org).

If you're antiquing, allow yourself some time to poke around the shops on the main street. Antiques hunters customarily go from Bedford Village on to Scotts Corners in **Pound Ridge,** which has not only several antiques shops but also quite a few antiques fairs and sidewalk sales. Many people call Pound Ridge the arts and antiques capital of Westchester. There are more than twenty shops and galleries, all within half a mile of one another. To reach Pound Ridge, follow Route 172 east out of Bedford Village, then turn right onto Route 137, then left onto Westchester Avenue. It'll take you right into Scotts Corners, a one-street village center usually lined with Mercedes-Benzes, BMWs, or limousines-in-waiting. Quite a few celebrities have or have had homes tucked away in the dense woods that ramble off in every direction around here.

DINNER   About fifteen minutes away, in nearby New Canaan, Connecticut (follow Route 124), there are a couple of restaurant options. **Gates Restaurant,** 10 Forest St. (203-966-8666; www.centroristorante.com/gates.htm), has burgers, salads, pasta, and seafood dishes. It's a lively and very popular meeting spot right between East and Locust Avenues.

LODGING   **The Roger Sherman Inn,** 195 Oenoke Ridge, New Canaan, CT (203-966-4541; www.rogershermaninn.com), sits on a lovely stretch of country road just outside the center of New Canaan (not quite a fifteen-minute drive from Scotts Corners; just follow Route 124). It's a small seven-room inn (some with fireplaces) that dates from ca. 1740.

DAY 2 / MORNING

BREAKFAST   A continental breakfast comes with the room at the **Roger Sherman Inn.**

From New Canaan backtrack through Scotts Corners and follow Route 124 to South Salem. **South Salem** is the kind of community where you may find yourself asking directions to the center of town, only to be told, "You're in it." It's made up of a post office, a library, a town hall, a police barracks, a market, two churches, and some beautiful old houses. To reach the center, take a right onto Route 35, and then turn left onto Spring Street. Spring Street runs right into Main Street, which is where "everything" is. Chances are good that you'll pass some horseback riders en route. There are several horse farms in South Salem, and all the roads are used for riding.

In nearby **Cross River** (which is about 2 or 3 miles west of South Salem, via Route 35), you'll find two of northern Westchester's most delightful attractions, the Yellow Monkey Village and Ward Pound Ridge Reservation. Yellow Monkey Village is a little cluster of 18th-century buildings colonized by chic shops selling everything from flowers to stylishly finished plumbing supplies and highly valued antiques. Each shop keeps its own hours.

LUNCH   If the weather's good, take a picnic to **Ward Pound Ridge Reservation.** Turn right when you pull out of the Yellow Monkey Village driveway and immediately turn right into the **Fifth Division** (788 Route 35; 914-763-3580), a little market/deli where you can gather picnic provisions.

AFTERNOON

Directly opposite the Fifth Division is Route 121. Right after you turn onto Route 121, you'll see a sign at the entrance of Ward Pound Ridge Reservation (914-864-7317; www.westchester gov.com/parks), a 4,700-acre nature preserve. Do yourself a big favor here and stick to the posted speed limit of a mere 15 miles per hour—you will drive away unticketed if you do. You can take your pick of places to park and wander the park's trails. They cut through meadows and woodlands and run alongside streams, up hillsides, through deep hemlock ravines, over marsh swamps, by cliffs—you name it. The Reservation, as the locals refer to it, is rife with birds and other wildlife. There's a small museum called the Trailside Museum with taxidermic mounts, a weather station, and Indian artifacts. Out back there's a wildflower garden. Any time of year is a beautiful time to visit the Reservation. In winter you can cross-country ski or go sleigh riding or tobogganing. Admission is $8 a car or $4 if you have a Westchester County Park Pass (open 8 a.m. to dusk). A map is provided.

After at least a couple of hours of fresh air, head back toward South Salem, turning left onto Mead Street (about 2 miles east of the Fifth Division) to go into **Waccabuc,** a very exclusive community with a country club as its centerpiece. As you drive up Mead, you'll pass one exquisite home after another. If you can't get enough of the beautiful homes, detour down Schoolhouse Road and you'll see more, though foliage hides a lot during the warm-weather months. Then continue back on Mead Street past the **Mead Street Chapel,** which is beautifully tucked away in a corner of the woods, practically blending into the scenery. To the right you'll spot Lake Waccabuc, which has private access only. Mead Street eventually runs into Hawley Road (which is also known as the Mountain Road). Turn left and then turn right onto 121. You are now in **North Salem,** which seems to have more horses than people. Everywhere you look you see farms, with jump-studded pastures and big old barns. You'll see Vox (the restaurant we've chosen for dinner) on the right, at the corner of Route 116. Turn right there and follow Route 116 into Ridgefield, Connecticut, where you can settle into your home for the night. It's just a short drive back to North Salem for dinner and for touring the next day.

DINNER   **Vox Bar & Restaurant,** at the junction of Routes 116 and 121; (914) 669-5450; www.voxnorthsalem.com. For many years, this corner was home to a landmark restaurant, Aubergege Maxine, which was owned and run by a French chef. His brother took over the establishment and continues to serve French cuisine. It's not quite as formal as the original restaurant was and the cuisine is more American and Nouveau French.

LODGING   **Elms Inn,** 500 Main St., Ridgefield, CT; (203) 438-2541; www.elmsinn.com. A historic inn, built in the 1760s. Guest rooms are furnished with some antiques and four-poster beds. Consider having a meal here as well, though reservations in advance are a must. The kitchen is run by Brendan Walsh, a former chef of Arizona 206.

DAY 3 / MORNING

BREAKFAST   Complimentary continental breakfast is served at the **Elms Inn.**

Return to North Salem, via Route 116, and you can fill several hours just taking in all the bucolic scenery. Be sure to stop and take a quizzical look at **Balanced Rock** (on Route 116, about a quarter of a mile away from Vox), which was left behind from the Ice Age. At the intersection of Routes 116 and 124, go straight on Titicus Road and then turn left onto Mill's Road, which takes you through beautiful countryside that looks more like something you'd expect to find in northern Vermont. At some point you can either turn around or carry on to Purdy's and then follow Titicus Road around the reservoir back to North Salem.

At Salem Center turn left and then turn right onto Deveau Road, which takes you up to the **Hammond Museum and Japanese Stroll Garden,** 28 Deveau Rd. (914-669-5033; www.hammond museum.org). The museum, which was founded by Natalie Hays Hammond in 1957, has a schedule of changing exhibits and activities, many focusing on the Far East. Out back there's a Japanese Stroll Garden. The Hammond and its garden are open from noon to 4 p.m. Wed through Sat, and Sun in July and Aug, from 11 a.m. to 3 p.m.

LUNCH **The Silk Tree Café** at the Hammond Museum, Deveau Road (914-669-6777), serves lunch in an elegant tree-lined courtyard from noon to 3 p.m. Wed through Sat. Reservations are strongly recommended.

AFTERNOON

Return to Route 124 and turn right. For more stunning scenery take the next right onto Baxter Road, which is one of North Salem's horsiest roads. Along the way you can park and walk (or ski or go horseback riding) on what is called the **North Salem Open Land Foundation,** which is open to the public and free.

Afterward, return to Route 124, turn right, and you'll soon come to the **Old Salem Farm** on the left. This handsome farm (which used to be owned by Paul Newman) is famed in the equestrian world for its shows, and it attracts horse lovers from around the country. For information on horse shows, visit www.oldsalem farm.net or call (914) 669-5610. Visitors are welcome year-round to walk through the stables and have a look around.

When you pull out of the farm, turn left onto Route 124 and follow it for a couple of miles until you come to Guinea Road on the left. Turn and follow that until you reach **Salinger's Orchard,** Guinea Road, Brewster (845-277-3521; www.salingersorchard .com). You'll know you're close when you start seeing apple trees on both sides of the road. Apples, however, are just part of the picture at Salinger's. Here you can get fresh-baked breads and pies, doughnuts, peanut butter, honey, pasta, and scores of other wonderful treats. Be forewarned, however, that during fall weekends the place is packed. The orchard is open from 9 a.m. to 5:30 p.m. year-round.

From Salinger's backtrack to Route 124 and follow it back to Hardscrabble Road on the right. A short distance in, on the left, is the **North Salem Vineyard** (914-669-5518; www.northsalemwine .com). Free tours and tastings are offered year-round, Sat and Sun from 1 to 5 p.m. The vineyard will prepare a basket lunch, which you can eat indoors or out.

From the vineyard you can very easily hop back on I-684, heading south toward New York City. You'll find the entrance by turning left out of the vineyard and following Hardscrabble Road, which crosses right over I-684.

There's More . . . .

See Southern New England Escape Two, Ridgefield and New Canaan.

Animal farm. **Muscoot Farm,** Route 100, Somers; (914) 232-7118; www.westchestergov.com/parks/muscootfarm.htm. This is a turn-of-the-20th-century interpretive farm owned and operated by the Westchester County Department of Parks, Recreation, and Conservation. From Katonah go west on Route 35 to Route 100 and turn right. The farm is 1½ miles down on the right.

Bicycling. Many of the roads in this area are great cycling routes, though quite hilly. Consider taking your bicycle along. An especially good biking area is **Ward Pound Ridge Reservation.**

Hiking. In addition to some of the hiking places already described, this part of Westchester has several wildlife preserves with nature trails. In Mount Kisco there are two sanctuaries worth seeking out. Both are havens for birders. The **Butler–Meyer Sanctuary** is a 363-acre preserve with self-guiding trails and a resident naturalist. This sanctuary is popular for birders; in fact, there is a hawk-watch station. To reach Butler: At Bedford Village bear left on Route 172 for 1 mile to the Shell station and the blinker (still on Route 172) and go 2 miles, under I-684; carry on another three-tenths of a mile up the hill, and just before you reach the top of the hill, turn left onto Chestnut Road; go 1½ miles and you'll see the entrance on the right. **Westmoreland Sanctuary** (www.westmorelandsanctuary.org), which is opposite Butler, offers 625 acres with 15 miles of trails to explore. There are also a museum, nature programs, naturalists, and guided walks. Another worthwhile preserve is **Halle Ravine,** a small (38-acre) area on Trinity Pass in Pound Ridge. It's very scenic with a gorge and stream.

Skiing. During the winter months you can cross-country ski in Ward Pound Ridge Reservation and on the Open Land Foundation property in North Salem.

Special Events . . . .

MAY

Horse Show, Old Salem Farm, Route 124, North Salem; (914) 669-5610; www.oldsalemfarm.net. Though there are horse shows throughout the year, this one is the biggest. It usually takes place the last two weeks in May. In addition to all the competitions, there are food stalls and vendors selling everything from curry combs to saddles and great Western wear.

Other Recommended Restaurants and Lodgings . . . .

BANKSVILLE

La Crémaillère, 46 Bedford–Banksville Rd.; (914) 234-9647; www .cremaillere.com. This French provincial restaurant—just a couple miles down the road from Bedford Village—is beautifully situated in a 1750s "Widow Brush House." It offers a wonderfully romantic atmosphere with brick fireplaces and murals throughout, as well as unfailingly good dishes such as its cassoulet of escargots, ravioli au fromage, roast duckling, and coquilles St. Jacques.

BEDFORD VILLAGE

Bistro Twenty-Two, Route 22, Bedford; (914) 234-7333; www.bistro 22.com. A sophisticated country restaurant, Bistro Twenty-Two is open for dinner Mon through Sat and for lunch Thurs, Fri, and Sat.

NEW CANAAN

Tequila Mockingbird, 6 Forest St.; (203) 966-2222. Here you'll find one of the most authentic Mexican restaurants in the Westchester–Fairfield County areas. In addition to wonderfully fresh south-of-the-border fare, you'll find splashy colors, paintings, and folk art.

RIDGEFIELD

Bernard's Inn at Ridgefield, 20 West Lane; (203) 438-8282; www
.bernardsridgefield.com. This small inn was purchased and completely refurbished by the dynamic cooking team, chefs Bernard
and Sarah Bouissou. Their nonpareil French cuisine can be enjoyed
inside elegant dining rooms or—during the summer months—in
the Victorian patio gardens.

Elms Inn, 500 Main St.; (203) 438-9206; www.elmsinn.com.
Owned by highly regarded American chef Brendan Walsh (the original chef of New York City's Arizona 206), the Elms Inn has earned
itself a wonderful reputation. There are several small dining rooms,
always abuzz with contented diners. Among the menu offerings:
Connecticut seafood stew, grilled loin of Cervena venison, and
thyme-roasted pheasant.

SOUTH SALEM

Le Château, Route 35; (914) 533-6631; www.lechateauny.com.
Some people have never heard of South Salem, but they've heard
about Le Château. The castle itself, built in 1907 by J. P. Morgan,
is on thirty-two woodland acres. The classic French cuisine is reliably good.

For More Information . . . .

New York State Division of Tourism, 30 Pearl St., Albany, NY
12245; (518) 474-4116 or (800) 225-5697; www.iloveny.com.

Putnam County Visitors Bureau, 110 Old Route 6, Carmel, NY
10512; (845) 225-0381 or (800) 470-4854; www.visitputnam
.org.

Westchester County Office of Tourism, 222 Mamaroneck Ave., White Plains, NY 10605; (800) 833-9282; www.westchestergov .com/tourism.

NEW YORK ESCAPE *Five*
Montauk and the Hamptons
LONG ISLAND BEACHES / 2 NIGHTS

Sun-bleached beaches. Platters piled high with spanking-fresh lobster. Sea-breeze-swept verandas. These are just some of the images that come to mind when you mention Montauk or the Hamptons to most New Yorkers. This strip of Atlantic coast on Long Island's eastern end has long been a favorite summer escape for city residents.

Ocean beaches and views
Fresh seafood
Chic boutiques
Museums
Estates
Historic houses
Horseback riding
Wildlife
Spa

Though sharing the same stretch of beach (it goes on for miles and miles), the Hamptons and Montauk are actually very different. The Hamptons, which include Westhampton, Hampton Bays, Southampton, Bridgehampton, and East Hampton, are very upscale, with huge houses surrounded by well-coiffed hedges. They are also very social, attracting celebrities and other bold-faced names from all over. Many New Yorkers either rent, own, or take shares in summer houses and spend a good chunk of their time party hopping or playing tennis with clients. Montauk, on the other hand, is more laid back in both appearance and attitude.

For this escape we combine a visit to both the Hamptons and Montauk. If you'd rather spend more time beaching, consider cutting the journey in half, visiting either just the Hamptons or just Montauk.

By the way, traffic can be painfully uncomfortable, especially going out on Friday afternoons and evenings and returning to the city on Sunday afternoons and evenings. Do yourself a big favor and

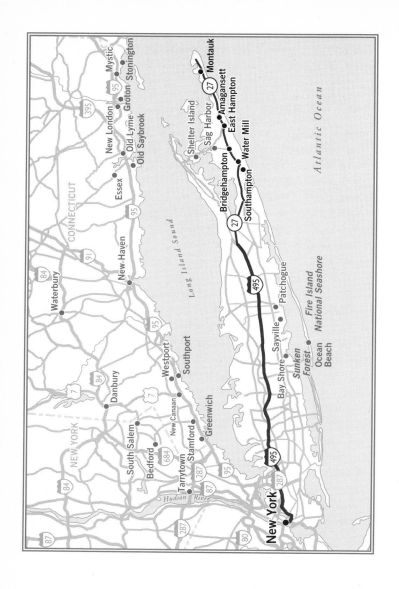

get a jump start on your trip. Leave early in the morning or mid-week. Also, bear in mind that many inns have a three-night mini-mum, and some have a one-week minimum during July and Aug.

DAY 1 / MORNING

Start by taking the Midtown Tunnel from Manhattan under the East River and follow the Long Island Expressway (I-495) east to exit 70. Follow the signs for Route 27 and then turn left. Route 27, the Sunrise Highway, takes you to the five towns known as "the Hamptons" and on to Montauk at the island's easternmost point.

All five of the Hampton towns have long been a haven for writers, artists, and other celebrities in addition to summer visitors. The main attraction is the beach, which, backed by rolling dunes, stretches out for miles, offering plenty of opportunity for undisturbed sunning.

As you hopscotch from town to town, you'll find that a popular Hamptons activity is browsing through the boutiques and galleries; in fact, sometimes it's hard to tell the difference. Here, a perfect ear of corn can be discussed as if it were an objet d'art, filling the better part of a dinner-party conversation. You'll find all sorts of one-of-a-kind must-haves such as heavy pasta bowls and conversation-piece sweaters that you'll figure out how to clean later. If you're here for the shopping, your best bet is to just pull over wherever you spot a parking place in a town. Chances are there will be enough shops to keep you happily amused.

Otherwise make your first stop in **Southampton** at the **Old Halsey House,** 249 South Main St. (631-283-3527). This is the oldest English frame house in New York State. There's also a colonial herb garden. The house has summer and off-season hours. Call in advance. Also worth seeing is the **Southampton Historical Museum,**

17 Meeting House Lane, off Main Street (631-283-2494; www.south hamptonhistoricalmuseum.org). The main building, which was formerly a whaling captain's home (1843), is filled with period furnishings. There's also a one-room schoolhouse and a carriage house plus a 19th-century village street with more than a dozen restored shops.

Southampton's most famous shopping area is **Job's Lane,** where you'll find pricey boutiques competing for your credit card signature. As riveting as shopping can be, don't miss the **Parrish Art Museum,** also on Job's Lane at 25 Job's Lane (631-283-2118; www.parrishart.org), which has a good collection of 19th- and 20th-century American paintings along with other changing exhibits. During the summer it's open Mon through Sat from 11 a.m. to 5 p.m. and Sun from 1 to 5 p.m.; closed Tues and Wed from mid-Sept. Closed some holidays.

After a look around the Parrish and a bit of shop hopping, take time out to gape at the town's legendary mega mansions. As with most affluent oceanfront areas, the biggest and the best homes are on the roads that run parallel to the ocean or intersect them. You can feast your eyes by driving down Meadow, Gin, Halsey Neck, Copper's Neck, and First Neck Lanes.

LUNCH **The Plaza Café** (61 Hill St., 631-283-9323; www.plazacafe .us/Plaza.html) really gets it right when trying to please the New Yorker crowd it caters to. Specializing in New American cuisine with lots of creatively prepared seafood, it's owned by chef Douglas Gulija.

AFTERNOON

Even if you're not a hard-core beach person, consider taking time out to plop down on the beach for an hour or so. There's a wonderful public beach right on Meadow Lane.

Afterward, continue east on Route 27, stopping at shops in the villages of **Water Mill** and **Bridgehampton.** Water Mill is named for its gristmill, which is now a museum called the **Water Mill Museum,** Old Mill Road (631-726-4625; www.watermillmuseum.org). It's open from Memorial Day through mid-Sept.

The destination for the day is **East Hampton,** which has an impressive collection of old houses that have been declared historic landmarks. The best way to enjoy them is to stop by the East Hampton Chamber of Commerce, 79A Main St. (631-324-0362; www.easthamptonchamber.com), and pick up a free walking-tour map. Some of the highlights include the oldest houses, some of which can be found on James Lane, which borders the eastern edge of the South End Burying Ground. Most famous of them is the 1680 **"Home Sweet Home" House,** 14 James Lane (631-324-0713; www.easthamptonchamber.com), which was the childhood home of John Howard Payne, the composer of the song of the same title. It's open to visitors Apr through Dec, 10 a.m. to 4 p.m. Mon through Sat and 2 to 4 p.m. Sun from Apr through Sept and Sat and Sun only in Oct and Nov. There's also a windmill that was built in 1804 out back. **Historic Mulford Farm,** ca. 1680, is also on James Lane (631-324-6850; www.easthamptonhistory.org). It's a living-history museum with summer hours only (call ahead).

On Main Street you'll find the **Guild Hall Museum,** 158 Main St. (631-324-0806; www.guildhall.org), which is an art museum and the cultural center of East Hampton. During the summer it's open Mon through Sat from 11 a.m. to 5 p.m. and Sun from noon to 5 p.m. In the winter, hours are Thurs through Sat from 11 a.m. to 5 p.m. and Sun from noon to 5 p.m. Close by you'll find **Clinton Academy,** 151 Main St. (631-324-6850; www.easthampton.com), the first prep school in New York State. It's now a museum exhibiting a collection of eastern Long Island artifacts. Call ahead; hours vary.

At the end of town on North Main Street stands **Hook Mill,** a wind-powered gristmill, next to a burial ground with tombstones dating from 1650. There are tours of the mill through the summer.

Before leaving East Hampton, take a drive down Lily Pond Lane to see more magnificent homes.

DINNER   **Nick & Toni's,** 136 North Main St. (631-324-3550; www .nickandtonis.com), prides itself on its wood-burning-oven specials. The cuisine is Mediterranean with lots of fresh fish on the menu.

LODGING   **The Maidstone Arms Inn and Restaurant,** 207 Main St. (631-324-5006; www.maidstonearms.com), is a nineteen-room inn across from the green in East Hampton. It dates back to the 17th century and keeps its doors open year-round.

DAY 2 / MORNING

BREAKFAST   During the summer months a full breakfast (included in the room rate) is served at the **Maidstone Arms Inn and Restaurant.** The rest of the year, a continental breakfast is available.

Amagansett is less than 3 miles from East Hampton and can be reached by following Route 27. Amagansett has more shops to explore plus the **Town Marine Museum,** on Bluff Road, one-half mile south of Route 27 on the ocean (631-267-6544; www.east hampton.com), with shipwreck and undersea exhibits. There are also several town beaches on which to spread your blanket out.

From Amagansett carry on east to Montauk, which is truly land's end. Though just 120 miles from the chasms and towers of Manhattan, it honestly feels a million miles away. You'll start to feel the difference just after Amagansett, when the shops trickle out.

There's not a long list of things to do in **Montauk.** The best pastime is to wander along the beach looking for shells or birds, or maybe go for a trail ride on a pair of mares at the **Deep Hollow Ranch,** located on Route 27 (3 miles east of Montauk) (631-668-2744; www.deephollowranch.com).

The one big sightseeing attraction is the **Montauk Point Lighthouse** in **Montauk State Park,** 6 miles east of town on Route 27 (631-668-2544; www.montauklighthouse.com), which has stood poised atop an ocean bluff for over 200 years. It was built in 1795 by order of George Washington.

LUNCH   **Gosman's Dock,** West Lake Drive at the entrance to Montauk Harbor (631-668-5330; www.gosmans.com), is famed for its generous servings of ultrafresh seafood (you can watch them unload catches right on the dock). Try the broiled fluke; it's hard to find elsewhere. You'll find a take-out counter and some picnic tables outside in addition to the restaurant dining rooms inside. (Gosman's is closed during the winter.)

AFTERNOON

Spend the afternoon exploring the trails of nearby **Hither Hills State Park,** 3 miles west on Route 27 (631-668-2554). The park is open year-round, sunrise to sunset.

DINNER   **Dave's Grill,** Flamingo Rd. on Montauk Harbor; (631) 668-9190; www.davesgrill.com. This formerly run-down fishermen's haunt is now a sophisticated bistro. Order the fish of the day or try the Provençal fisherman's stew out on the waterside patio.

LODGING   **Montauk Yacht Club Resort and Marina,** Star Island (631-668-3100; www.montaukyachtclub.com), is a deluxe hotel complete with tennis, water sports, spa treatments, and lots more. Back in the twenties and thirties, it was frequented by the Vanderbilts, Astors, and Whitneys.

DAY 3 / MORNING

BREAKFAST   A buffet breakfast is set up at the **Montauk Yacht Club Resort and Marina,** when they're open (between Apr and Nov). The buffet starts early, at 7 a.m.

After breakfast consider spending the day being pampered at **Gurney's Inn Resort & Spa,** Old Montauk Highway (631-668-2345; www.gurneys-inn.com), before heading back to Manhattan.

To return to the city, retrace your steps by following Route 27 west and turning north at Eastport to reach the Long Island Expressway (I-495), which will take you back to the Midtown Tunnel.

There's More . . . .

Biking. **Amagansett Beach & Bicycle,** at the light in Amagansett, 624 Montauk Hwy. (631-267-6325; www.amagansettbeachco.com), has all types of bikes (kids' cruisers, hybrids, mountain bikes, and tandems) for rent. Locks and helmets are included.

Birding. **Montauk Point State Park** is a good spot to take your binoculars.

Fishing. In Montauk, charter boats will take anglers out to fight for blues, marlin, swordfish, and even sharks.

Horseback riding. **Deep Hollow Ranch** in Montauk offers horseback riding through 4,000 acres of trails to the beach. For more information call (631) 668-2744; www.deephollowranch.com.

Spa. **Gurney's Inn Resort & Spa,** Old Montauk Highway, Montauk; (631) 668-2345; www.gurneys-inn.com. In addition to a long menu of spa treatments (seaweed body wraps, herbal wraps, facials, massages), Gurney's is home to a gorgeous beach the likes of which you'd be hard-pressed to find anywhere else.

Special Events . . . .

JULY 4TH
Southampton's Parade. The town's antique-auto museum shows off its classic cars in an annual parade.

LABOR DAY WEEKEND
Powwow at the Shinnecock Indian Reservation, just off Route 27A (near Southampton). Dances, ceremonies, displays.

Other Recommended Restaurants and Lodgings . . . .

AMAGANSETT
Clam Bar, 2025 Montauk Hwy.; (631) 267-6348. Open from May through Oct, this is the place to go to for fresh seafood. The menu includes the catch of the day whether it's fresh tuna, swordfish, or striped bass. Their menu also features lobster, clam chowder, scallops, fried clams, oysters, and clams on the half shell. Dress is supercasual. Diners eat under yellow and white umbrellas outside or at the counter. Service is quick.

Lobster Roll, 1980 Montauk Hwy. (look for flagpole); (631) 267-3740. In summer months this is a must. A no-frills, roadside seafood eatery, its lobster sandwiches and salads are worth every minute you stand in line. There are also wonderful pies for dessert.

EAST HAMPTON

Babette's, 66 Newtown Lane; (631) 329-5377; www.babetteseast hampton.com. Here you can feast on wonderfully healthy cuisine. Many fitness-minded celebs have dined here, including Gwyneth Paltrow, Jerry Seinfeld, Richard Gere, and Ed Burns.

Della Femina, 99 North Main St.; (631) 329-6666; www.della femina.com. Popular in the Hamptons since the early 1990s, Della Femina prides itself on its creative New American dishes.

Laundry, 31 Race Lane; (631) 324-3199; www.thelaundry.com. Go if only to try the jumbo lump crab cakes with avocado salsa. Laundry is locally famed for its seafood and imaginative American dishes.

Maidstone Arms Inn and Restaurant, 207 Main St.; (631) 324-5006; www.maidstonearms.com. The food here is contemporary American with a Pacific Rim influence. Among its star-studded clientele are Billy Joel, Alec Baldwin, Kim Basinger, Steve Guttenberg, and Kevin Costner—just to drop a few names.

Riccardo's Seafood House, 313 Three Mile Harbor Rd.; (631) 907-1000. Along with dramatic sunsets, the cuisine here is dreamy: Latin seafood specialties. In fact, the ceviche alone is worth the trip.

MONTAUK

Montauk Manor, 236 Edgemere St.; (631) 668-4400; www.montauk manor.com. An English Tudor-style castle, Montauk Manor originally was erected by industrialist Carl Fisher as the centerpiece for what he had hoped to be an elaborate summer resort community. Unfortunately, the Great Depression squelched his plans. Nevertheless, the building remains, renovated inside to be a modern luxury hotel. Ask for a room with a terrace or patio.

The Panoramic View, 272 Old Montauk Hwy. (631-668-3000; www.panoramicview.com), lives up to its name. It's spectacularly situated on ten acres with arrestingly beautiful ocean vistas. The rooms are simply but tastefully decorated with maple furniture. They have high, beamed ceilings and knotty-pine paneling; most have balconies.

SOUTHAMPTON

Red Bar Brasserie, 210 Hampton Rd.; (631) 283-0704; www.red barbrasserie.com. An East End favorite, this restaurant serves up French-inspired American fare. The signature dish is pan-seared sea scallops with creamed corn, fava beans, and black trumpet mushrooms.

Savanna's, 268 Elm St.; (631) 283-0202. Locally famed for its creatively prepared American dishes, including seafood and some Southern style cuisine. Keep in mind, however, Savanna's is not open during the winter months.

Village Latch Inn Hotel, 101 Hill St.; (631) 283-2160; www .villagelatch.com. Steps away from Southampton Village, this sixty-seven-room inn is comprised of charming buildings, both historic and contemporary. It's an easy walk to the area's beaches, shops, restaurants, galleries, and museums.

For More Information . . . .

East Hampton Chamber of Commerce, 79A Main St., East Hampton, NY 11937; (631) 324-0362; www.easthamptonchamber.com.

Hamptons Online, P.O. Box 299, Southampton, NY 11969; (631) 287-6630; www.hamptons.com.

Long Island Convention and Visitors Bureau, 330 Motor Parkway, Suite 203, Hauppauge, NY 11788; (631) 951-3440; www.licvb .com.

Montauk Chamber of Commerce, P.O. Box 5029, Montauk, NY 11954; (631) 668-2428; www.montaukchamber.com.

New York State Division of Tourism, 30 Pearl St., Albany, NY 12245; (518) 474-4116 or (800) 225-5697; www.iloveny.com.

NEW YORK ESCAPE *Six*

Shelter Island
A TOTAL GETAWAY / 1 NIGHT

If you want to go someplace for the weekend and just "be" rather than "do," Shelter Island is a good choice. Tucked between the north and south forks on the east end of Long Island, it's reachable only by

> Beaches
> Seafood
> Biking
> Peace and quiet

ferry. About a third of the island is nature preserve (Mashomack), and the rest is beautifully unspoiled, thanks to residents who are committed to keeping it that way.

Some say the name Shelter Island comes from an Indian word; others say it was named by Quakers who were persecuted by the Puritans in New England and sought refuge there. Whatever. There is a monument to the Quakers and a graveyard with 17th-century stones if you're interested. That's about it in the way of man-made attractions on the island. The island's real attraction is its natural beauty: miles of white-sand beaches, rolling wooded hills, and lots of beautiful views of the water.

To avoid the summer traffic, plan to head out to the island between May (except Memorial Day weekend) and early June or after Labor Day through Oct (except for Columbus Day weekend).

Consider combining this trip with a visit to Montauk or the Hamptons (see New York Escape Five).

DAY 1 / MORNING

From Manhattan take the Queens/Midtown Tunnel to the Long Island Expressway (I-495). Follow it out to exit 70 and pick up Route 27

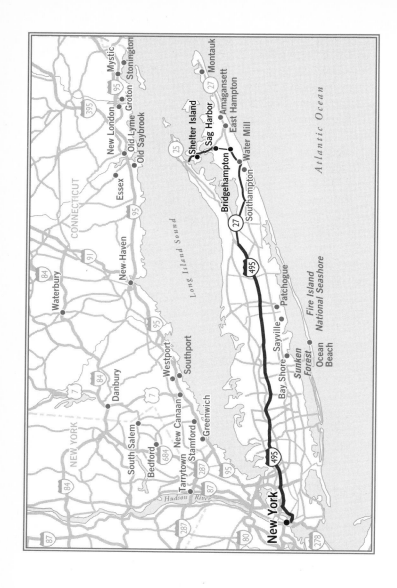

east; turn left in Bridgehampton following signs to Sag Harbor. From downtown Sag Harbor cross the bridge and follow signs to the ferry. Ferries shuttle between North Haven and Shelter Island several times throughout the day. For information, call (631) 749-1200 or visit www.southferry.com. The price for one car with a driver is $12 each way. Round-trip, same-day tickets are $15. There are also ferries from Greenport on the North Fork (www.northferry.com).

Once you arrive on Shelter Island, follow Route 114 to **Shelter Island Heights,** where you'll find the island's handful of stores and restaurants, including the Chequit Inn, where you can take time out for lunch.

LUNCH   **Chequit Inn,** 23 Grand Ave. (631-749-0018; www.shelter islandinns.com), has a terrace from which you can gaze out at sailboats in Dering Harbor. The restaurant specializes in grilled seafood, though lighter fare is available at lunch.

AFTERNOON

After lunch and maybe a short walk around the Heights, head to the eastern tip of the island, where you'll find a causeway leading to Ram Island, so named because it's shaped like a ram. Check into your hotel and spend the afternoon parked on its private beach or swinging in a hammock under a shady tree in the backyard. If you feel ambitious, the hotel has a tennis court to play on and sailboats to take out. You can also rent bikes (or take along your own) and do some pedaling around this 12-square-mile island.

DINNER   **The Ram's Head Inn,** 108 Ram's Island Dr.; (631) 749-0811. This restaurant, where reservations are a must, alone is worth the trip to Shelter Island. The cuisine is contemporary American, and the setting (it overlooks Coecles Harbor) is dreamy.

LODGING   The Ram's Head Inn (www.shelterislandinns.com) is marvelously situated in a whole little world of its own. All seventeen rooms are nothing extraordinary (though they're perfectly adequate) but are more than compensated for by the setting.

DAY 2 / MORNING

BREAKFAST   Continental breakfast is included in the room rate at the Ram's Head Inn.

Enjoy the morning on the beach, then grab a ferry back to **Sag Harbor,** which is an old whaling town filled with 19th-century architecture and history. In fact, tiny Sag Harbor used to rival New York as an international port. There are a handful of sights to see, including the **Custom House,** Main and Garden Streets (631-692-4664; www.splia .org), which operated as a customhouse and post office during the late 18th and early 19th centuries. It was actually the first customs house established by an act of Congress, in 1789, and has been restored by the Society for the Preservation of Long Island Antiquities. From June through Sept it's open Tues through Sun. On the corner of Garden Street and Main, you'll find the **Sag Harbor Whaling and Historical Museum,** Garden and Main Streets (631-725-0770; www .sagharborwhalingmuseum.org), which tells the story of the island's whaling past. The museum is open daily from mid-May through Sept.

LUNCH   A Sag Harbor must, the **American Hotel,** 25 Main St. (631-725-3535; www.theamericanhotel.com), is renowned for its old world charm. The food is largely American French.

From Sag Harbor head back to Bridgehampton and retrace your steps back to New York City.

There's More . . . .

Bicycling. On Shelter Island you can rent bikes at **Piccozzi's,** right in the center of the Heights on Bridge Street; (631) 749-0045.

Hiking. The **Mashomack Preserve,** off Route 114 on Shelter Island, covers one-third of Shelter Island. It has trails and a visitor center and is open daily. The entrance is marked by a large wooden sign on the east side of Route 114, 3 miles south of the Greenport/North Ferry landing. For more information call (631) 749-1001 or visit www.shelter-island.org and click on Mashomack Nature Preserve.

Special Events . . . .

JUNE
Shelter Island 10K Run and Race Walk. This is always an exciting day on Shelter Island, when athletes come from all over to race. It starts in the center of the island near the high school.

AUGUST
Arts and Crafts Show. Every year the playground near the American Legion in the center of the island turns into a showcase for artists and artisans.

Other Recommended Restaurants and Lodgings . . . .

SAG HARBOR
The Beacon, 8 West Water St.; (631) 725-7088; www.beacon sagharbor.com. This is a wonderful spot to settle in and watch the boats glide by. The menu features imaginative salads, the freshest seafood, and perfectly grilled rib-eye steaks.

SHELTER ISLAND
Azalea House, 1 Thomas Ave.; (631) 749-4252; www.azaleahouse bedandbreakfast.com. This is a five-room bed-and-breakfast in the island's center. Thanks to one of its owners, who comes from Finland, it's full of tasteful Finnish touches including light-pine furniture. An extended continental breakfast is included in the room rate.

SHELTER ISLAND HEIGHTS
The Dory, Route 114; (631) 749-8871; www.doryrestaurant.com. This is a busy waterfront restaurant (with a dory on top) where the seafood is unfailingly good. It's necessary to have reservations during the summer months.

For More Information . . . .

Long Island Convention and Visitors Bureau; (631) 951-3440; www.licvb.com.

New York State Division of Tourism, 30 Pearl St., Albany, NY 12245; (518) 474-4116 or (800) 225-5697; www.iloveny.com.

Sag Harbor Chamber of Commerce, at the foot of Main Street in the Windmill, Sag Harbor, NY 11963; (631) 725-0011; www.sagharbor chamber.com.

Shelter Island Chamber of Commerce, P.O. Box 577, Shelter Island Heights, NY 11965; (631) 749-0399; www.shelter-island.org.

NEW YORK ESCAPE *Seven*

Fire Island—With or Without a Car

LIFE'S A BEACH / 1 NIGHT

Nicknamed New York's Key West, Fire Island has long been known as a carefree, barefoot kind of place, attracting an interesting cross section of humanity. Its occupants are made up of the

> Beaches
> Seafood
> Nature walks
> People-watching

year-rounders, summer-home owners, summer renters, and short-term visitors including day-trippers.

A barrier island stretching 32 miles along the southern side of Long Island and only a quarter-mile wide, Fire Island has a rich social and cultural history. Resort development began here back in the 1890s with the establishment of a Chautauqua Assembly, a movement for Christian betterment through learning and the arts. After that tracts of land were bought up by developers and sold to city folk who were seeking vacation lots. Before long the island became a patchwork of neighborhoods for different communities, often overlapping and coexisting harmoniously, whether involved in boating, fishing, family, or gay life.

Fortunately, the island hasn't changed much since its early days. No cars were allowed then—or now. The only means of transportation are feet, wagon, bicycle, and boat (golf carts and trucks for contractors). Though only 40 miles from New York City, it is a remote destination with wonderfully wide sandy beaches and unspoiled maritime forests. Most of the land is now protected by the federal government and has been designated the Fire Island National Seashore. Keep in mind that many hotels and restaurants close for the cold-weather months.

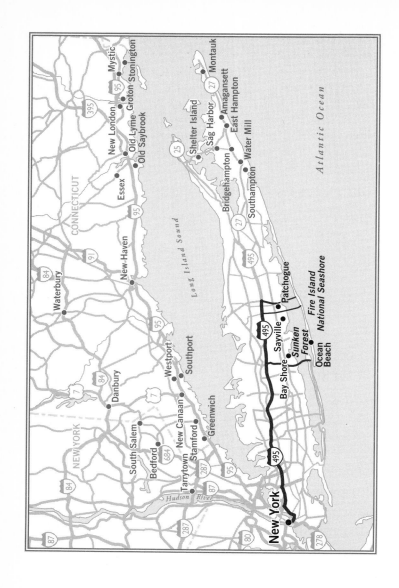

There are several ways to reach the island from Manhattan if you don't have a car. You can take either the Long Island Rail Road or a jitney to the ferries at Bay Shore, Sayville, or Patchogue. You can also take a taxi from Manhattan (without spending a fortune) to Bay Shore Ferry. If you're driving your own car, take the Long Island Expressway to exit 53 for Bay Shore, exit 59 for Sayville, or exit 63 for Patchogue. There's a parking field at the ferry dock with daily charges. See "Getting There" at the end of this escape for more details.

DAY 1 / MORNING

Once on the island, you'll find the largest concentration of hotels and restaurants in **Ocean Beach,** Fire Island's de facto capital. Don't, however, wait very long before making hotel reservations on summer weekends. The rooms, especially, fill quickly.

LUNCH You can have a simple seafood sandwich, a burger, or a salad under an umbrella outside at **Maguires on the Bay** (Bay Number 1, Bungalow Walk, Ocean Beach; 631-583-8800; www.maguiresbayfrontrestaurant.com).

AFTERNOON

After lunch relax a bit on your hotel's beach and then head over (by foot or bike) to take a walk at the **Sunken Forest** (631-589-0810; www.nps.gov/fiis), a National Park Service site in Sailors Haven. The Sunken Forest is truly a sight to behold. It is made up of thirty-six acres of dense trees and vines and laced with a boardwalk.

DINNER **Matthew's Seafood House** (on the bay, east side of Ocean Beach; 631-583-8016; www.matthewsseafood.com) is a good choice for . . . you guessed it! Seafood. It has been an island favorite for more than thirty years.

LODGING   **Seasons,** 468 Denhoff Walk, Ocean Beach; (631) 583-8295; www.fivacations.com. This little B&B is open year-round and has seven rooms (with shared baths) and a one-room cottage.

DAY 2 / MORNING

BREAKFAST   Breakfast (included in room rate) at **Seasons.**

After breakfast head over by the water taxi to **Watch Hill** (631-597-6455; www.nps.gov/fiis), the island's other National Park Service site, which is about 7 miles east of the Sunken Forest. Situated between the bay and the ocean, Watch Hill is made up of wild salt marsh and dense groves of pitch pine and holly and is lovely to walk around.

Then return to Ocean Beach and plant yourselves on the beach until lunch.

LUNCH   **Albatross** (Bay Walk, Ocean Beach; 631-583-5697) has patio tables that make great perches for people-watching.

After lunch check out the current exhibit at the **Ocean Beach Historical Society** (Bayview and Cottage Walks, Ocean Beach; 631-583-8972). Hours are Thurs through Mon from 10 a.m. to 2 p.m. and 7 to 10 p.m. Closed from Labor Day through June.

Later, after more sun and relaxation or perhaps a bike ride (by the way, the Seasons provides bikes for your use), head back to the mainland and Manhattan.

There's More . . . .

Lighthouse. The **Fire Island Lighthouse** (Fire Island National Seashore; 631-661-4876; www.fireislandlighthouse.com) is located on the western end of Fire Island. You can go to the visitor center in the keeper's quarters next to the 19th-century lighthouse. Hours vary seasonally. For tour information, visit the Web site.

Walking. Besides Watch Hill and the Sunken Forest, there are several wonderful walks on Fire Island. There's a 7-mile walk from Watch Hill east to Smith Point, a 7-mile boardwalk trail at Smith Point, and a 4-mile walk east from Smith Point to Moriches Inlet.

Special Events . . . .

JULY AND AUGUST
Beach Apparatus Drills. Every third Thurs at 7 p.m., a group of dedicated volunteers reenacts drills performed by the U.S. Lifesaving Service at the turn of the 20th century to rescue shipwreck victims from stranded ships. Takes place in front of the lighthouse. Parking is at Robert Moses Field #5.

Other Recommended Restaurants and Lodgings . . . .

OCEAN BEACH
Clegg's Hotel, 478 Bayberry Walk; (631) 583-5399; www.cleggs hotel.com. Directly across from the ferry dock, this very simple (not luxurious) hotel was built in the 1920s by the grandfather of the current proprietor.

For More Information . . . .

Fire Island National Seashore, 120 Laurel St., Patchogue, NY 11772, (631) 289-4810; www.nps.gov/fiis. South of Montauk Highway, off West Avenue.

New York State Division of Tourism, 30 Pearl St., Albany, NY 12245; (518) 474-4116 or (800) 225-5697; www.iloveny.com.

Getting There. . . . .

By train: The Long Island Rail Road provides daily service from Pennsylvania Station to Bay Shore, Sayville, and Patchogue, where you can catch a ferry. The trains leave every thirty to sixty minutes. The ferry terminal at Patchogue is within walking distance of the railroad station, and the ferries at Bay Shore and Sayville are a short taxi ride away. The Long Island Rail Road also offers packages that include the train and ferry. For information visit www.lirr.org or call (718) 217-5477 or (516) 822-5477.

By van: Tommy's Taxi has a van shuttle service that takes you from 68th Street and Third Avenue to the Bay Shore ferry. Departures from Manhattan are from 8 a.m. to 9 p.m. daily, from Apr through the end of Oct. Fares are approximately $22 one-way Mon through Sat and $25 one-way on Sun and holidays. For more information call (631) 665-4800.

By ferry: For current ferry fares and schedules, contact Fire Island Ferries, (631) 665-3600; www.fireislandferries.com.

NEW YORK ESCAPE *Eight*
The Adirondack Area
TOWNS AND COUNTRY / 3 NIGHTS

Look at any color map of New York State and you'll see an enormous green area taking up a good chunk of its northern region. That's the Adirondack Park, the largest natural preserve in the East, in fact, covering some six million acres (or 9,375 square miles).

Backwoods wilderness
Thoroughbred racing
Performing arts
Museums
Family amusements
Lakes
Old fort
Hiking
Canoeing

You could easily spend weeks here, dividing your time between the different fresh-air activities (including hiking through birch and balsam forests and paddling canoes on lakes) and poking around the attractions near Lake George and in nearby Saratoga Springs, or you could devote an entire week or two to an all-out vacation on a hidden mountain lake.

For this trip we combine a brief visit to Saratoga Springs with a short stay on Lake George and Blue Mountain Lake. All three places could be weekend (or longer) destinations in themselves; we've just mentioned the highlights. Keep in mind that in Aug, when the New York Racing Association has its equine competitions, Saratoga Springs' population swells to two or three times its normal size.

DAY 1 / MORNING

Take I-87 north to exit 13N. Go left. At the fourth stoplight turn left into **Saratoga Spa State Park** in Saratoga Springs, which is home to your hotel for the night.

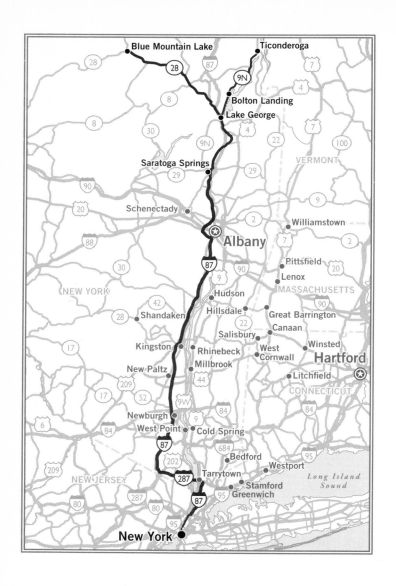

Saratoga Springs, a town with a beautiful mixture of Victorian and Greek Revival architecture in the foothills of the Adirondack Mountains, has three major magnets: its thoroughbred racing, its performing arts scene, and its mineral baths, for which the town is named. If you'd like to try the latter, you'll find some right in the park—at the **Roosevelt Bath and Spa** (518-226-4790; www.gideon putnam.com). Here you can "take the waters" or, more specifically, soak in naturally carbonated water ("nature's champagne") and follow with a massage or other spa treatment. The experience should leave you feeling relaxed and revived and ready to get out and wander around the town's museums and shops. Hours vary throughout the year; call in advance.

LUNCH　　　　The dining room of the **Gideon Putnam Hotel,** in Saratoga Spa State Park, 24 Gideon Putnam Rd. (518-584-3000; www.gideonputnam.com), is a pleasant spot to have lunch. A large variety of offerings includes burgers, sandwiches, crepes, and the like.

AFTERNOON

Spend the afternoon checking out the sights and shops in town (follow US 9 north into town from the park). Many of the shops on Broadway are in buildings that have been impeccably restored to their original Victorian appearance. On North Broadway, Circular Street, and Union Avenue, there are many mansions that were originally built in the 1800s. Be sure to wander into historic **Congress Park,** on Broadway (518-584-6920), which is home to the Saratoga Springs History Museum (www.saratogaspringshistorymuseum .org) and the Walworth Memorial Museum. They trace the history of the city's growth. From June through Sept they're open daily 10 a.m. to 4 p.m.; Oct through May, Wed through Sat 10 a.m. to 4 p.m. and Sun 1 to 4 p.m. Closed January.

If you're interested in the history and highlights of horse racing, be sure to check out the **National Museum of Racing and Thoroughbred Hall of Fame,** 191 Union Ave. (518-584-0400; www.racingmuseum.org). It's open Mon through Sat from 10 a.m. to 4:30 p.m. and Sun from noon to 4 p.m. And, of course, there's the **Saratoga Race Course,** also on Union Avenue, which is the oldest operating thoroughbred racetrack in the country (it was founded in 1863). For information on events, call (518) 584-6200 or visit www.nyra.com.

If you have time, try to visit Saratoga's wonderful dance museum, the **National Museum of Dance and Hall of Fame,** at 99 South Broadway in Saratoga State Park (518-584-2225; www.dancemuseum.org). It's the only museum in the country devoted exclusively to professional American dance. It's open between the end of June and mid-Oct, Tues through Sun from 10 a.m. to 5 p.m.

DINNER **Olde Bryan Inn,** 123 Maple Ave. (518-587-2990; www.oldebryaninn.com) is the place to go to get a big, hearty meal. Dinner offerings include almond-encrusted salmon, Cajun blackened steak, and New Orleans pasta.

LODGING **The Gideon Putnam Hotel,** in Saratoga Springs State Park, half a mile south of town on Route 9, is one of Saratoga Springs' grande dame hotels, surrounded by therapeutic pools, tennis courts, and golf courses. Legendary Sunday brunches take place here in glass-walled rooms overlooking the greens.

DAY 2 / MORNING

BREAKFAST During race season (end of July and Aug), a great way to start the morning in Saratoga is by having breakfast at the track (for information call **Breakfast at Saratoga,** 518-584-6200). A buffet is served from 7 to 9:30 a.m., during which you can watch the early-morning workouts. A more formal champagne breakfast is offered during racing season in a dining tent called **At the Rail Pavilion** (call 518-584-6200 for restaurant information). Otherwise, in downtown, head for **Beverly's,** 47 Phila St. (518-583-2755), where you can get German apple pancakes, eggs Benedict, and other delicious dishes.

After breakfast head north on I-87 to exit 20 and follow Route 9 north, which will take you through the commercialized town of **Lake George** (shops, entertainment arcades, family attractions) and to **Bolton Landing,** where you can settle in for an all-out relaxing stay at the lakefront Sagamore resort. (See "Lodging," below) Check-in time is not until 3 p.m., but the front desk will hold your bags while you have lunch.

LUNCH   **Mister Brown's Pub** at the **Sagamore,** 110 Sagamore Rd. (518-644-9400; www.thesagamore.com), is an informal spot where you'll find soups and salads, sandwiches, and burgers.

AFTERNOON

Spend the afternoon enjoying the resort facilities at the Sagamore or drive up to see **Fort Ticonderoga,** the military fortress and its museum (follow Route 9N to Ticonderoga; 518-585-2821; www .fort-ticonderoga.org).

Afterward, follow the scenic drive up to the top of **Mount Defiance.**

DINNER   **La Bella Vita** at the Sagamore, 110 Sagamore Rd. (518-743-6101; www.thesagamore.com) is a great choice, offering Northern Italian cuisine in an elegant setting. Also at the Sagamore, you'll find **The Club Grill,** which specializes in steak (518-743-6101 for reservations).

LODGING The Sagamore, (800) 358-3585. Established more than one hundred years ago, this Victorian landmark has been described by just about every travel writer as a grande dame hotel. Indeed it is. In addition to one hundred guest rooms and suites in the main building, there are Lakeside Lodges with wood-burning fireplaces and private terraces and all sorts of sports and activities year-round.

DAY 3 / MORNING

BREAKFAST A huge buffet is offered at the **Sagamore.**

To sample some of the Adirondack's most densely scenic landscape, head west on Route 28, making your destination **Blue Mountain Lake,** where there's an outstanding museum devoted to the Adirondacks. Set on the shores of Blue Mountain Lake, the **Adirondack Museum,** Routes 28N and 30 (518-352-7311; www .adirondackmuseum.org), is a complex of twenty-two buildings on thirty acres. One of the most popular exhibits is a display of the successive generations of Adirondack boats. The museum is open 10 a.m. to 5 p.m. daily between mid-May and mid-Oct. It is closed one day in Sept, the day before the Rustic Fair takes place (second weekend in Sept).

AFTERNOON

LUNCH At the Adirondack Museum, there is the **Lake View Café** with a "million-dollar view." You can get salad, soup, chili, sandwiches, and entrees or stop in the grocery store in town and get picnic fixings to take on a hike up Blue Mountain.

The head of the trail leading to the summit (3,800 feet) is about 1½ miles north of town. The 3-mile-long hike will take you through dense Adirondack scenery.

DINNER Big family-style meals, with homemade breads and desserts, are served in the dining room at **Hemlock Hall,** on Route 28N (518-352-7706). Open from Memorial Day through mid-Oct.

LODGING At **Hemlock Hall** on Route 28N (518-352-7706 or, in winter, 518-359-9065; www.hemlockhall.com), you can stay in a motel-like unit, a lodge room, or a cabin on the lake. Open from Memorial Day through mid-Oct.

DAY 4 / MORNING

BREAKFAST Pancakes, hot cereals, eggs with bacon or sausage—big American breakfasts (included in the room rate) are served in the dining room at **Hemlock Hall.**

Before heading back to New York City, take time to enjoy the lake and its exquisite scenery. Right at the hotel you can take your pick of canoes, sailboats, paddleboats, and rowboats.

From Blue Mountain Lake retrace your steps back on Route 28 to I-87, heading south.

If you have even more time (another day or two), consider heading farther north up to the **Lake Placid** area. You can visit several Olympic attractions, including the Olympic Sports Complex, Ski Jumps, and the **1932 & 1980 Lake Placid Winter Olympic Museum,** Main Street (518-523-1655; www.orda.org), which includes video highlights of the 1932 and 1980 games, athletes' uniforms, sports equipment, and other Olympic memorabilia. All around the area you'll find lots of hiking and mountain-biking trails.

Come winter, there's every kind of snow and cold-weather sport imaginable—from skating and skiing to bobsled riding and luge rocket rides.

There's More . . . .

Hiking. The High Peaks of the Adirondacks are in this region. There are 46 peaks, most rising over 4,000 feet with hiking trails throughout. Trail maps and information is available at the **Adirondack Mountain Club** centers in Lake George and Lake Placid. For planning in advance, visit www.adk.org/home-flash.aspx.

Mountain biking. **High Peaks Cyclery: Mountain Adventure Center,** 331 Main St., Lake Placid; (518) 523-3764; www.highpeaks cyclery.com. Here you can rent mountain bikes and be sent on your way, choosing anything from an easy 10-mile rolling-hill route to a 75-mile loop with steep ascents. The adventure center can also set you up for in-line skating, skating, camping, and rock climbing.

Performing arts. **Saratoga Performing Arts Center,** Saratoga Spa State Park, Saratoga Springs; (518) 587-3330; www.nadeaumusic .net/saratogaperformingartscenter.html. The center hosts a wonderful summer mélange of cultural events, including the New York City Opera in June, the New York City Ballet in July, and the Philadelphia Orchestra in Aug, as well as concerts by a variety of rock, pop, folk, and jazz artists.

Polo matches. **Saratoga Polo Association,** Saratoga Springs; (518) 584-8108; www.saratogapolo.com. Matches take place in Aug.

Scenic drives. Phenomenal scenery is certainly not hard to come by in this part of the world, but for the most outstanding views, take the 8-mile-long climb, known as Whiteface Mountain Veterans Memorial Highway, from the crossroads in Wilmington to the summit of the fifth-highest Adirondack mountain.

Scenic flights. Adirondack Flying Service, Lake Placid Airport, Route 73, Lake Placid; (518) 523-2473; www.flyanywhere.com. Twenty-minute aerial tours are offered. Passengers can opt for the High Peaks Tour or the Whiteface Mountain Tour; $30 per person (minimum two people).

Skiing. The Adirondacks are home to about a dozen alpine ski centers, including **Whiteface Mountain** in Lake Placid (www.whiteface .com), and **Gore Mountain** (www.goremountain.com), which has three mountains for skiing and riding. Additionally, there are dozens of Nordic touring centers. At www.adk.com, the official guide to the Adirondacks, you'll find lists and links to the areas. Also check out www.crosscountryskinewyork.com.

Steamboat rides. The **Lake George Steamboat Company** offers narrated cruises on the lake. For information, call (518) 668-5777 or visit www.lakegeorgesteamboat.com.

Waterfalls. The **High Falls Adventure Center** (4761 Route 86, Wilmington; 518-946-2278; www.highfallsgorge.com) has walkways and groomed paths taking you alongside (and over on sturdy footbridges) the AuSable River, which tumbles its way over ancient granite cliffs.

Special Events . . . .

JUNE
Lake Placid Horse Show, Lake Placid. This show, combined with the I Love New York Horse Show held the first week of July, make the Adirondack area a popular destination for equestrians.

No-Octane Regatta, Blue Mountain Lake. A grand parade of boats. Events include War Canoe Race, Hurry Scurry Race, Guideboat Race, Jousting Competition, Paddling Races, Sailing Canoe Races, and Great Versatility Race.

JULY
Ticonderoga Memorial Military Tattoo, Fort Ticonderoga. Eighteenth-century military music in honor of the Scots who served here.

SEPTEMBER
Adirondacks National Car Show, Lake George Village. Hot rods, custom-made cars, and other special-interest cars are paraded here annually at the Fort William Henry Motor Inn.

Rustic Furniture Fair, the Adirondack Museum, Blue Mountain Lake. This annual fair showcases one-of-a-kind works by sixty craftspeople. Second weekend in Sept.

Other Recommended Restaurants and Lodgings . . . .

CHESTERTOWN
Friends Lake Inn, 963 Friends Lake Rd.; (518) 494-4751; www .friendslake.com. Just across the road from Friends Lake, this is a seventeen-room inn. All rooms are decorated in a country motif; some have four-poster beds. The restaurant is very well respected

for its sophisticated cuisine and award-winning wine list. Come winter, there are snowshoe trails and a cross-country-ski loop right behind the inn.

LAKE PLACID

High Peaks Resort, 2384 Saranac Ave.; (518) 523-4411; www .highpeaksresort.com. Located right in town, the High Peaks Resort has 133 rooms, several with fireplaces, whirlpool tubs and direct waterfront access to Mirror Lake. Their Reflections restaurant—with great outdoor dining offering views of the mountains and lakes—is a must, showcasing the talents of Executive Chef Charles Brucculeri (formerly of the Bryant Park Grill).

Lake Placid Lodge, 144 Lodge Way, (877-523-2700; www.lake placidlodge.com). One of the most elegant hotels in the Adirondacks, this Relais & Châteaux property is stunningly set on the shores of Lake Placid. Guests can stay in lakeside cabins or in lodge suites.

Mirror Lake Inn, 5 Mirror Lake Dr.; (518) 523-2544; www.mirror lakeinn.com. Propped up on the shores of Mirror Lake, this handsome resort and spa is within easy walking distance of the town of Lake Placid's shops, restaurants, and attractions. There are 128 rooms, including some with oversize whirlpool baths, private balconies, and lofts with king-size beds.

The Paradox Lodge, 2169 Saranac Ave.; (518) 523-9078; www.para doxlodge.com. A real find for both dining and lodging, the Paradox Lodge is a green Victorian house that was built in 1899 and later completely renovated. All eight of its rooms are beckoningly decorated with handcrafted Adirondack furniture, voluminous comforters, colorful quilts, and clawfoot tubs in the bathrooms. Some have water views. For dining, the chalkboard specials of the day always include some spankingly fresh fish prepared by the chef/owner.

The Whiteface Lodge, 7 Whiteface Inn Lane; 800-903-4045; www .whitefacelodge.com. This magnificent Great Camp-style resort has eighty-five guest suites with Adirondack furnishings, gas fireplaces, and some very exciting common areas, including a fifty-six-seat Surround Sound movie theater, ten-pin bowling lanes, an indoor and outdoor pool, and a year-round outdoor skating rink. Its Kanu restaurant, which is three stories high and grandly designed with Great Camp-era furnishings, is the setting for hearty, hand-crafted meals—lots of native fish and game dishes—prepared in an exhibition kitchen.

NORTH RIVER
Garnet Hill Lodge; (518) 251-2444; www.garnet-hill.com. For Nordic skiers, life doesn't get much better than this. You can stay in the main log-house lodge or one of the other buildings scattered around the woods. The cross-country trail system, right outside the door, includes 55 kilometers of groomed trails through pinch-me-it-can't-be-real scenery.

NORTHVILLE
The Lapland Lake Nordic Vacation Center, 139 Lapland Lake Rd.; (518) 863-4974; www.laplandlake.com. Situated in the south-central region of the Adirondacks, this is a year-round woodsy escape that's ideal for families. Guests stay in simple Finnish-style tupas, which are cottagelike accommodations. Come winter, it's a cross-country skier's dream, with fifty kilometers of trails groomed for classic and skate skiing. Lapland Lake was founded about three decades ago by Olavi Hirvonen, a former U.S. Olympic cross-country skier. Along with his wife, Ann, he continues to run it today.

SARANAC LAKE
The Point, Beaverwood Road; (518) 891-5674 or (800) 255-3530; http://thepointresort.com. Located in the northern Adirondacks on an isolated peninsula on Upper Saranac Lake, the Point was built in 1933 as a country getaway for William Avery Rockefeller. Constructed of massive logs and stone, it is a very exclusive retreat with eleven guest rooms, each with a fireplace and museum-quality Adirondack furniture. Extraordinarily good meals are served in the Great Hall, a spectacular high-ceilinged room with hunting trophies adorning the walls.

SARATOGA SPRINGS
Adelphi Hotel, 365 Broadway; (518) 587-4688; www.adelphi hotel.com. A grand old Victorian hotel. Complimentary continental breakfast is served in your room.

Inn at Saratoga, 231 Broadway; (518) 583-1890; www.theinnat saratoga.com. A very simple, historic hotel within easy reach of Saratoga's attractions.

For More Information . . . .
Adirondack Regional Tourism Council, P.O. Box 2149, Plattsburgh, NY 12901; (518) 846-8016; www.visitadirondacks.com.

Lake George Chamber of Commerce, Route 9, Lake George, NY 12845; (518) 668-5755 or (800) 705-0059; www.lakegeorge chamber.com.

Lake Placid/Essex County Visitors Bureau, 216 Main St., Lake Placid, NY 12946; (518) 523-2445; www.lakeplacid.com.

New York State Division of Tourism, 30 Pearl St., Albany, NY 12245; (518) 474-4116 or (800) 225-5697; www.iloveny.com.

Saratoga Springs Chamber of Commerce, 28 Clinton St., Saratoga Springs, NY 12866; (518) 584-3255; www.saratoga.org.

Warren County Tourism Municipal Center, 1340 Route 9, Lake George, NY 12845; (518) 761-6366 or (800) 365-1050; www .visitlakegeorge.com.

NEW ENGLAND
ESCAPES

NEW ENGLAND ESCAPE *One*

Lower Fairfield County

EXPLORING THE GOLD COAST / 2 NIGHTS

> Magnificent homes and
>   estates
> Marine life
> Antiques and crafts shops
> Beaches

Big old Victorian houses on golf courselike lawns, estates poised on the shores of Long Island Sound, tidal rivers swollen with yachts and sailboats. This little chunk of Connecticut, colonizing the state's southwestern corner, is home to a small galaxy of prosperous towns.

Unfortunately, many would-be visitors skip over the whole area, assuming it's a pocket of bedroom communities. Indeed, thanks to its proximity to New York (most of the towns can be reached in less than an hour), many of its residents commute into the city daily; nevertheless, lower **Fairfield County** is a good fit for a weekend escape. Within the span of two days, you can hopscotch from town to town (including Greenwich, Norwalk, and Westport), sampling exceptionally good restaurants and discovering truly top-notch museums and shops. On top of that you'll find plenty of opportunities to wander around in gardens, in woodland preserves, and along the shore.

Many of the communities along the coast were established in the 1700s, when the area was a thriving commercial center. Most of them are linked by the Boston Post Road (which dates back to the 18th century), also known as US 1 and frequently referred to as the Boston Post Road, Old Post Road, or simply the Post Road. To confuse visitors even more, Route 1 has a variety of other names in various communities it passes through on the East Coast between the states of Maine and Florida. Its original purpose—to connect the communities and provide food and lodging for weary travelers

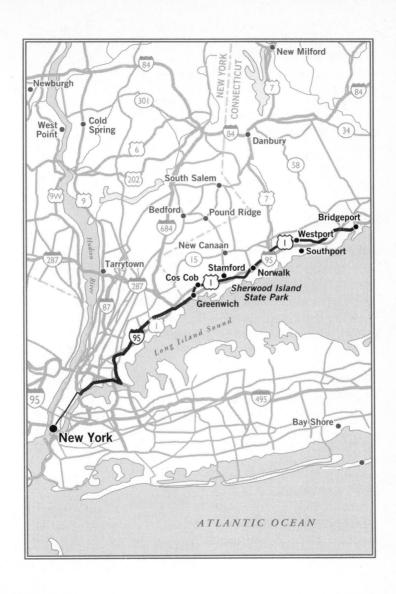

along the way—is still very much alive, though in a modern-day version. Along the way you'll pass big-name stores like Staples and Stew Leonard's as well as fast-food chains, gas stations, movie theaters, and the usual assortment of suburban retailers.

DAY 1 / AFTERNOON

If you want to do as the locals do, skip out of Manhattan early on a Fri afternoon to beat the rush-hour traffic. Make your destination **Greenwich** (a mere 28 miles from Times Square, I-95, exit 3), which is the first town you come to when entering the state from the southwest.

DINNER   Chef-owned **Restaurant Jean-Louis,** 61 Lewis St., between Mason Street and Greenwich Avenue (203-622-8450; www.restaurantjeanlouis .com), is a splurgey but well-worth-it choice. For gourmet chef Jean-Louis needs no introduction: He is widely acclaimed for unfailingly good French cuisine, for which he combines both classical and contemporary techniques. Don't even think of not making reservations. To reach the restaurant, turn left off exit 3 onto Arch Street; cross Greenwich Avenue and then turn left onto Mason Street. Lewis Street is the second street down on the left.

LODGING   **The Homestead Inn,** 420 Field Point Rd. (203-869-7500; www.homesteadinn.com), is a fully restored 1799 farmhouse mansion beautifully designed with stunning furnishings and linens. It is a Relais & Châteaux property and is home to the Thomas Henkelmann Restaurant.

DAY 2 / MORNING

BREAKFAST   Guests at the Homestead Inn can have a delicious full breakfast in the **Thomas Henkelmann Restaurant.** Afterward, devote the morning hours to exploring the town itself, which is centered on Greenwich Avenue, making up an easily strollable historic district complete with wide streets, historic buildings, and stone churches. The shops, of which there are many and all kinds, especially on Greenwich and Putnam Avenues, are on the pricey side (with some exceptions, such as the consignment shops).

Plan to visit the **Putnam Cottage,** 243 East Putnam Ave. (203-869-9697; www.putnamcottage.org), which was known as Knapp's Tavern during the Revolutionary War and was a meeting place of leaders including General Israel Putnam. The building itself, which dates from ca. 1690, is an attraction (the rare scalloped shingles are especially noteworthy), but indoors there are exhibits as well. It's open very limited hours, so call ahead.

Allow plenty of time to tour the **Bruce Museum,** 1 Museum Dr. (203-869-0376; www.brucemuseum.org). It's a museum of art and science, with exhibits changing about four times a year. It's open year-round from 10 a.m. to 5 p.m. Tues through Sat and 1 to 5 p.m. Sun. Afterward, consider driving around the country roads of Greenwich, which are punctuated with massive estates, especially along Lake Avenue, North Street, and Round Hill Road. Many peer out from behind high stone walls, crisp white fences, and iron gates.

In nearby Cos Cob you'll find the **Bush–Holley House,** 39 Strickland Rd. (203-869-6899; www.hstg.org), a National Historic Landmark (1732) that was originally the home of David Bush, a successful farmer and mill owner. Later, from 1890 to 1925, it was a boardinghouse, owned and operated by the Holley family, where writers and artists gathered. Hours vary; call ahead. Afterwards, head to **Stamford,** by hopping on I-95 (exit 7) or following the Post Road east.

LUNCH In Stamford, join the regulars at **Bull's Head Diner**, 43 High Ridge Rd. (203-961-1400), which boasts a nine-page menu of mainstream favorites, including lots of Greek specialties.

AFTERNOON

Stamford is home to more than several Fortune 500 corporations, which have colonized its forest of very new-looking office towers. It's also home to several worthwhile attractions such as the **Stamford Museum and Nature Center,** 39 Scofieldtown Rd. (203-322-1646; www.stamfordmuseum.org), a 118-acre site that includes a New England working farm, trails, galleries, and a planetarium. It's open Mon through Sat from 9 a.m. to 5 p.m. and Sun from 11 a.m. to 5 p.m. Also in Stamford is a unique fish-shaped church designed by Wallace K. Harrison. The **First Presbyterian Church,** 1101 Bedford St. (203-324-9522; www.fishchurch.org), was built in 1958; its stained-glass windows are by Gabriel Loire of Chartres, France. The **Stamford Historical Society Museum,** 1508 High Ridge Rd. (203-329-1183; www.stamfordhistory.org), has permanent and temporary exhibits, primarily on local history.

One of Stamford's most popular attractions, as well as a one-of-a-kind shopping experience, is **United House Wrecking,** 535 Hope St. (203-348-5371; www.unitedhousewrecking.com), which purveys the spoils of demolitions and estate sales (antiques, architectural items, old lighting and plumbing fixtures—you have to see this place). It's open year-round, Mon through Sat from 9:30 a.m. to 5:30 p.m. and Sun from noon to 5 p.m.

Once you've "done" Stamford, get back on I-95 and take exit 15 to get to **Norwalk.** Norwalk has a very pronounced maritime feel to it. It's home to an exceptionally informative maritime museum, which is called, not surprisingly, the **Maritime Aquarium at Norwalk,** located at 10 North Water St. (203-852-0700; www.maritime aquarium.org) in SoNo (South Norwalk). Half an hour in this place and you'll have a healthy respect for Long Island Sound and Norwalk's busy harbor life. Among its highlights: an aquarium with sharks and seals, an IMAX theater, a boatbuilding demonstration, and several interactive displays. Walk out the door and you're a couple of blocks away from SoNo's thriving epicenter, which is crammed with funky galleries, boutiques, and a selection of restaurants and bars. SoNo is a revitalized 19th-century seaside neighborhood listed on the National Register of Historic Places. Another truly worthwhile attraction in Norwalk is the **Lockwood–Mathews Mansion Museum,** 295 West Ave. (203-838-9799; www.lockwood mathewsmansion.com), a sixty-two-room Victorian mansion built by financier LeGrand Lockwood. By the way, the mansion was used as the nefarious Men's Association in both the 1975 and 2004 versions of the film *The Stepford Wives.* Hours are limited, so do call ahead. Sharing the same driveway is the **Stepping Stones Museum for Children,** 303 West Ave. (203-899-0606; www.steppingstones museum.org). This museum is a children's dream, with everything from a room where they can do endless water experiments to a full-size helicopter and train car in which they can fiddle with all the knobs and gadgets. Beyond the museum's parking lot, you'll find Devon's Place, a sprawling playground that was designed as a model of safety and accessibility. Children with physical, mental, and sensory challenges can use it as well as typically able youngsters. It's open daily, sunrise to sunset.

Plan to overnight in **Westport,** a town about which one resident summed up beautifully: "If you live in Westport, you don't have to go away to vacation." Indeed, the town, which is a summer weekend escape for many New Yorkers, has a resort feel to it, especially in the warm-weather months. The easiest way to reach it from Norwalk is to follow Saugatuck Avenue.

Turn right onto Riverside Avenue and follow it for less than half a mile to the Bridge Street Bridge, which is noteworthy only in that it's fabulously redundant. Cross over the Saugatuck River and take a look out at the water. Chances are good (between late Mar and mid-Nov) that you'll see rowers. The **Saugatuck Rowing Club**

(521 Riverside Ave.; 203-221-7475; www.saugatuckrowing.com) is a major presence in town, with rowing programs for students, masters, and Olympic-bound athletes. Turn right onto Compo Road South, which puts you in the **Compo Beach** neighborhood. As you approach the water, you'll suddenly begin to feel as if you've been miraculously transported to Nantucket, Martha's Vineyard, or some other idyllic seaside community, especially on a sunny day. You see physically fit people of all ages walking designer dogs, balancing on in-line skates, zipping along (clad in brightly colored Spandex) on bikes, or cruising in antique cars and shiny new convertibles.

Carry on east of Compo Beach to the **Greens Farms** area, which is home to one megahome after another especially along Beachside Avenue. By the way, if you have bikes to take along, this is a great biking route. Beachside Avenue takes you right into **Southport,** one of Connecticut's most picturesque communities. It's filled with Federal, Greek Revival, and Victorian houses and a couple of very grand churches. The best way to enjoy it is to park your car by the harbor and just wander around.

DINNER   Be sure to make reservations at the **Dressing Room** (27 Powers Ct., adjacent to the Westport Country Playhouse; 203-226-1114; www.dress ingroomhomegrown.com). The restaurant was founded as a partnership between the owner Michel Nischan, one of the most highly respected chefs in the world of organic, natural, and farm-direct food, and the late Paul Newman, who lent his name and support to it. Among the menu items are some wonderful American originals such as Yankee pot roast and Hook and Line Caught Chatham Cod.

The Dressing Room is adjacent to the **Westport Country Playhouse,** 25 Powers Ct. (203-227-4177; www.westportplayhouse.org), which has been a Westport landmark since 1931. This theater, which was recently completely rebuilt and dramatically enhanced, has had many a name on its stage, including Bette Davis, Helen

Hayes, and Paul Newman. Newman's wife, Joanne Woodward, was the theater's artistic director for several years.

The **Westport Arts Center,** 51 Riverside Ave. (203-222-7070; www.westportartscenter.org), showcases the works of Westport (and other) artists in its setting on the banks of the Saugatuck River. The gallery is open from 10 a.m. to 4 p.m. Mon through Fri and noon to 4 p.m. Sat and Sun. The center also hosts many concerts, film series, and children's programs throughout the year. During the summer months there are free concerts at the **Levitt Pavilion for the Performing Arts** (off Jesup Road, behind the Westport library; 203-226-7600; www.levittpavilion.com).

LODGING   The Westport Inn, 1595 Post Rd. East (203-259-5236; www .westportinn.com) is within easy reach of all of Westport's attractions.

DAY 3 / MORNING

BREAKFAST   If you want a light breakfast, head down toward the train station, in an area known as Saugatuck, where you'll find **Doc's Café** (570 Riverside Ave.; 203-226-9444), a popular gathering spot for many locals. There's a great selection of coffees and teas plus simple healthy breakfasts and lunches along with some yummy baked goods.

Afterward, take a walk around the center of town, which has been called a "mall without walls" because of the number of shops—many of them parts of major chains, including Ann Taylor, J. Crew, Williams-Sonoma, and a sprawling Banana Republic. In addition, you'll find some antiques shops in this part of town as well as along the Post Road.

If you're a bird-watcher, consider parking yourself on a bench along the banks of the Saugatuck River by the Westport Public

Library. During migration seasons you may see more exotic birds here in half an hour than some people see in a lifetime. This is also a good place to watch the rowers from the aforementioned Saugatuck Rowing Club.

LUNCH   A local institution, **Tavern on Main** (146 Main St.; 203-221-7222; www.tavernonmain.com) is the reliable standby for many Westporters. Indeed, it has roots in the community going back to the 18th century. For cold days, its low-beamed ceilings and wood-burning fireplaces are warm and welcoming; for hotter days, there's a terrace for alfresco dining.

After lunch head over to **Sherwood Island State Park** (right off exit 18 on what's called the Sherwood Island Connector; 203-226-6983; www.friendsofsherwoodisland.org) or back to Compo Beach for a day at the beach. Sherwood Island State Park is a 238-acre public playground where you'll pay for parking, $20 weekdays and $30 on weekends. Compo Beach, which local residents have access to by purchasing season passes, is open to non-residents, for $40 on weekends and holidays, $20 on weekdays. It is free during the off-season (Oct 1 to Apr 30). Or head into town to visit the **Westport Historical Society,** 25 Avery Place (203-222-1424; www.westporthistory.org). It includes a Victorian house (ca. 1795) with period rooms and exhibit spaces focusing on local history and famous residents over the years. There's also an octagonal-shaped barn in which a walk-around diorama of Westport in the year 1900 is featured. Call ahead for hours. You might also stop by **Earth-place: The Nature Discovery Center,** 10 Woodside Lane (203-227-7253; www.earthplace.org), a sixty-two-acre wildlife sanctuary with a museum in Westport.

To return, hop back on I-95 to get back to New York City.

There's More . . . .

In nearby **Bridgeport** you'll find the **Barnum Museum** (820 Main St.; 203-331-1104; www.barnum-museum.org), the **Beardsley Zoological Gardens** (1875 Noble Ave.; 203-394-6565; www.beardsleyzoo.org), the **Ballpark at Harbor Yard**, home of the Bridgeport Bluefish (500 Main St.; 203-345-4800; www.bridgeportbluefish.com), the **Discovery Museum** (4450 Park Ave.; 203-372-3521; www.discoverymuseum.org), and more—worth extending your trip for.

Nature walks. Look at a map of Fairfield County and you'll see green patches everywhere. It's home to quite a few nature preserves, including the following:

Audubon Center of Greenwich, 613 Riversville Rd., Greenwich (Route 15, exit 28; 203-869-5272; www.greenwichcenter.audubon.org), is a must for bird-watchers. It's a 522-acre sanctuary with 15 miles of woodland trails.

Barlett Arboretum, at 151 Brookdale Rd. off High Ridge Road (1 mile north of Route 15, exit 35), in Stamford; (203) 322-6971. Here you'll find sixty-three acres of natural woodland and gardens to explore.

The **Nature Conservancy's Devil's Den Preserve,** 33 Pent Rd., Weston; (203) 226-4991. Wander through 1,746 acres woven with more than 20 miles of well-marked trails through predominantly deciduous forests.

Sheffield Island Lighthouse can be reached by ferry from Hope Dock, which is at the corner of Washington Street and North Water Street in Norwalk. The lighthouse, which dates from 1868, has four levels and ten rooms to explore and is surrounded by three acres of prime picnic grounds. Boat trips and tours are offered between

Memorial Day and Oct. Call (203) 838-9444 for daily ferry service or visit www.lighthouse.cc/sheffield.

***Stargazing.* Rolnick Observatory,** 182 Bayberry Lane, Westport; (203) 227-0925; www.was-ct.org/wasobs.htm. Two nights a week, Wed and Thurs (or by appointment), the public can take in a free view of the night sky via a powerful telescope. Operated by Westport Astronomical Society.

Special Events . . . .

JUNE

Hidden Garden Tour, Westport. The Westport Historical Society hosts this annual event that allows visitors to tour magnificent gardens. For information, call (203) 222-1424 or visit www.westport history.org.

LATE JULY THROUGH EARLY AUGUST

Pequot Library Book Sale, Southport. This is the largest book sale in the state of Connecticut. It features more than 90,000 volumes in 45 categories and attracts more than 10,000 people. For more information, call (203) 259-0346 or visit www.pequot library.com.

AUGUST

SoNo Arts Celebration, Washington Street in South Norwalk. A big block party with food, crafts, arts, and entertainment; www.sono arts.org.

SEPTEMBER

Norwalk Oyster Festival, Veterans Park, Norwalk. This annual event celebrates Long Island Sound's seafaring history with entertainment, arts and crafts, boat trips, oyster shucking, and lots of foods; www.seaport.org.

Septemberfest, Greenwich Common, Greenwich. Carnival rides, entertainment, international food festival, a pet show, and more; www.unitedway-greenwich.com.

DECEMBER
Holiday House Tour, Westport. Every year, five of this community's houses are open for touring. The event is presented by the Westport Historical Society. For information, call (203) 222-1424 or visit www.westporthistory.org.

Other Recommended Restaurants and Lodgings . . . .

FAIRFIELD
Ash Creek Saloon, 93 Post Rd.; (203) 847-7500. If you're in the mood for ribs, head for this spot. It's famed for its cowboy offerings.

Centro, 1435 Post Rd.; (203) 255-1210; www.centroristorante .com. A great choice for dinner, Centro attracts a beautiful-people crowd who come for the pasta, gourmet pizzas, and other reliably good dishes. You can also count on good, chewy bread and olives for appetizers. There is also a Centro in Darien and one in Greenwich.

Firehouse Deli, 22 Reef Rd.; (203) 255-5527. Packed at lunch-time, this is where everyone (local businesspeople as well as Fair-field University and Sacred Heart students) goes to get a deli lunch. It's a converted firehouse dating from 1893. There's dining in the rear as well as sidewalk tables out front when the weather's good.

NORWALK

Lime Restaurant, 168 Main St.; (203) 846-9240; www.limeres taurant.com. While it has become a magnet for those seeking vegetarian cuisine this small spot actually offers a great selection of chicken, fish, and beef dishes. Servings are wonderfully generous.

ROWAYTON

The Restaurant at Rowayton Seafood, 89 Rowayton Ave.; (203) 866-4488; www.rowaytonseafood.com. Immaculately fresh seafood is prepared at this waterfront restaurant. Don't even think of showing up without reservations. It's a lot of people's favorite.

WESTON

Cobb's Mill Inn, 12 Old Mill Rd.; (203) 227-7221; www.cobbsmill inn.com. Housed in an 18th-century mill, this restaurant draws a large sentimental crowd who has traditionally been coming for holidays, birthdays, anniversaries, and other occasions. Though the food is not remarkable, the view—of the pond and waterfall—and the atmosphere are every bit Fairfield County.

WESTPORT

Blue Lemon Restaurant, 7 Sconset Sq.; (203) 226-2647; www .bluelemonrestaurant.com. Westporter foodies are regulars here. The food—which is creative American cuisine—is unfailingly good.

Riverview Restaurant, Saugatuck Rowing Club, 521 Riverside Ave.; (203) 227-3399; www.saugatuckrowing.com. Many Westporters know that while the restaurant at the rowing club is technically open to members and their guests only, you can snag a lunch or dinner reservation simply by dropping a name of a member you know (and if you don't know anyone, there are ways around it—such as introducing yourself to someone in the reception area). Well worth the white lie, as this restaurant is among the best in town. Its executive chef, Daniel Salomon, prepares American dishes using a variety of French and Italian accents. The setting is dreamy—looking out on the Saugatuck River with white sparkling boats and the leafy shoreline.

Splash Restaurant and Bar, Inn at Longshore, 260 South Compo Rd.; (203) 454-7798; www.decarorestaurantgroup.com. Located on the grounds of Longshore Club, which is basically a country club for Westport residents, this very popular spot is set on the shores of Long Island Sound. The cuisine is California–Asian and best enjoyed by ordering family-style platters to share.

Tuttis, 599 Riverside Ave.; (203) 221-0262. This is a wonderfully casual spot where you can sit down and feast on an impeccably good and imaginatively prepared pasta dish or other Italian-influenced entree.

For More Information . . . .

Coastal Fairfield County Convention and Visitors Bureau, 297 West Ave., Norwalk, CT 06850; (203) 853-7770 or (800) 866-7925; www.coastalct.com.

Connecticut Tourism Division, 505 Hudson St., Hartford, CT 06106; (860) 270-8080 or (800) 282-6863; www.ctbound.org.

NEW ENGLAND ESCAPE *Two*

Ridgefield and New Canaan

TWO TOWNS TO TOOL AROUND / 1 NIGHT

Historic villages
Stately homes
Antiques and crafts shops
Rural countryside

Not too many towns can say they have a gourmet sidewalk hot-dog vendor. Well, Ridgefield can. Right in the heart of town, at Chez Leonard's cart, you can take your pick of a variety of gourmet hot dogs, including Le Hot Dog Alsacienne (with sauerkraut, French mustard, and caraway seeds), Le Hot Dog Suisse (with Swiss fondue cheese), Le Hot Dog Mexicaine (with chili and Bermuda onions), and Le Hot Dog Excelsior Veneziano (sautéed peppers, onions, olives, tomatoes). Chez Leonard's hot-dog stand is not the only place in town with "good taste," however. The whole village, with its wide Main Street lined with buildings that range from pre-Revolutionary to Victorian, epitomizes good taste. There are no major interstates, parkways, or railroads that take you right there, which may have something to do with the town's wonderful unblemished quality. Nevertheless, as lovely as Ridgefield is, it has been growing quickly; in fact, many longtime residents talk about how beautiful it "used to be."

Less than half an hour's drive away is New Canaan, which is also an attractive residential community. The two are just over the New York border, less than 60 miles from Manhattan in the southwest corner of Connecticut. Together they make up a simple but charming weekend getaway with plenty of shops, restaurants, and scenery to keep you happily busy.

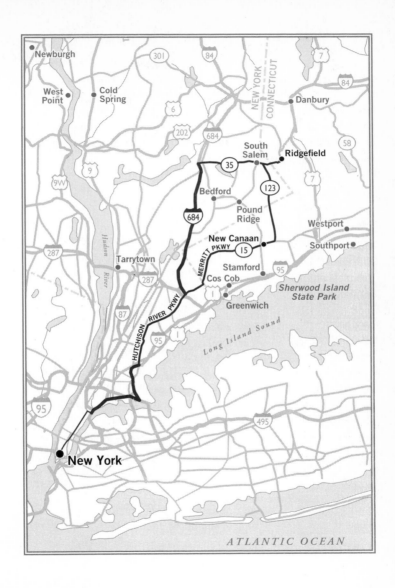

DAY 1 / MORNING

If you start out early in the morning, you'll have the whole day to poke around Ridgefield's shops and galleries. The drive should take no more than an hour and a half. Though there are several ways to get there, we recommend taking I-684 north and getting off at the Katonah/Cross River exit. Turn right and follow NY 35, which becomes CT 35 and takes you right into Ridgefield. If you have more time, consider combining this trip with our Northern Westchester escape (New York Escape Four). The two fit together beautifully.

Once you get to **Ridgefield,** start by grabbing a parking spot (there are a lot behind the Ridgefield Bank and Town Hall) and then set out to explore by foot. The hub of town can best be seen by walking down one side of Main Street (starting at the corner of Market Street, opposite St. Stephen's Church) to **Ballard Park,** then returning on the opposite side. Though it's just a 2- or 3-block walk, allow yourself plenty of time to meander in and out of the shops. As quaint as Ridgefield may be, it did experience a major war event back in 1777. After the British had landed in what is now Westport, they moved inland to Danbury. After burning it, they returned to their ships, passing through Ridgefield, and the Battle of Ridgefield broke out. You'll see evidence of this in town, including a couple of tablets commemorating the event and an actual cannonball embedded in the frame of the Old Keeler Tavern.

If it's a beautiful day, you may want to take a couple of Leonard's hot dogs into Ballard Park, which is a lovely green with lots of inviting benches. Or grab a table at **Fifty Coins** at 426 Main St. (203-438-1456; www.fiftycoinsrestaurant.com). Salads, burgers, wraps . . . it's a lively family place.

AFTERNOON

After lunch wander up the street to the **Aldrich Museum of Contemporary Art,** 258 Main St. (203-438-4519; www.aldrichart.org), which has changing exhibits along with a sculpture garden that elicits all sorts of puzzled looks and "Is this really art?" kinds of comments.

From the museum it's a fifteen-minute walk (or couple-minute drive) to the **Keeler Tavern Museum,** 132 Main St., at the junction of Routes 33 and 35 (203-438-5485; www.keelertavernmuseum .org). Here you can learn all about the town's history, which has its roots in colonial times, when it was a way station on the carriage road between New York and Boston. The Keeler Tavern (which dates from 1715) was an inn providing accommodations for the carriage passengers. Now it's a museum complete with guides dressed in period costumes. One of its most noticeable features, however, is a cannonball lodged in a wall. During the Battle of Ridgefield (1777) in the Revolutionary War, it was "sent" by the British.

To see a small but impressive collection of some of Ridgefield's most stunning homes, detour over to High Ridge Road (from the Keeler Tavern head west on Route 35, turn right onto Parley, and then right onto High Ridge). These magnificent homes, surrounded by flawless lawns, are especially attractive during the year-end holidays, when each one vies for your attention with wreaths adorning every window.

DINNER   You'll have a most memorable meal at the **Elms Inn,** 500 Main St.; (203) 438-2541; www.elmsinn.com. The menu revives the American Revolution with stews, spoon breads, and game meats. It's under the guidance of chef/owner Brendan Walsh.

LODGING   **Elms Inn** is a historic inn, originally built as a home in 1760. Guest rooms are furnished with some antiques and four-poster beds. The kitchen is one of the best in Fairfield County.

DAY 2 / MORNING

BREAKFAST   Guests at the **Elms** are served continental breakfast in their rooms, so seize the opportunity to relax and enjoy it.

Once you're up and about, set out for New Canaan, which you can easily reach by simply following Route 35 west. Just after you cross the New York border, turn left onto Route 123. Several miles down you'll cross the border again, into New Canaan. This route takes you through serenely scenic landscapes, passing horse farms, a golf course, and quite a few megahomes.

New Canaan, the center of which you can reach by turning right onto Locust Avenue, is a spick-and-span residential community where most residents look as though they could model for a Ralph Lauren catalog. This is Connecticut just as you pictured it. The side streets are lined with large multichimneyed houses with wraparound porches, graceful columns, and the kind of gardens you see featured in glossy magazines.

New Canaan is home to the **Silvermine Guild Arts Center,** 1037 Silvermine Rd. (203-966-9700; www.silvermineart.org), which is an art school with galleries showcasing the works of member artists and artisans. There is also the **New Canaan Historical Society,** 13 Oenoke Ridge Rd. (203-966-1776; www.nchistory.org), which oversees the original town hall, library, and drugstore, among other buildings. Both of these facilities have limited visiting hours, so call ahead.

If it's a beautiful day, take time out to walk around the **New Canaan Nature Center,** 144 Oenoke Ridge Rd. (203-966-9577; www.newcanaannature.org). Here there are more than forty acres of woodland, meadows, and ponds plus gardens and hands-on exhibits.

Before heading back consider stopping at **Gates Restaurant,** 10 Forest St. (203-966-8666), for a cup of cappuccino and a quick bite. Then return to Route 123, which will take you back to the Merritt Parkway for your return trip home.

There's More . . . .

Crafts. **Brookfield Craft Center,** 286 Whisconier Rd., Brookfield; (203) 775-4526; www.brookfieldcraftcenter.org. About fifteen minutes away from Ridgefield, this craft center is worth a detour. Here you'll find a school for craftsmanship, an exhibition gallery, and a gift shop. It's located in a historic gristmill complex on Route 25, just east of the four corners intersection with Routes 7 and 202, a few miles north of I-84.

Mall shopping. The **Danbury Fair Mall** (www.danburyfairmall.com) is not far from Ridgefield (follow Route 7 north). It has all the big stores—Macy's, Lord & Taylor, Sears—as well as a variety of food vendors.

Sightseeing flights. Scenic small-plane rides can be scheduled at the **Danbury Municipal Airport** through the Danbury Flight School. Trips generally start at about $75 each for a half-hour flight (based on two people). For information, call (203) 743-3300.

Special Events . . . .

MID-MAY THROUGH MID-JUNE
Art of Northeast USA Exhibition, Silvermine Guild Arts Center, 1037 Silvermine Rd., New Canaan; (203) 966-5617; www.silver mineart.org. A juried competition with paintings, drawings, and sculpture by participants from the Northeast states.

JUNE THROUGH SEPTEMBER
Chamber Music Festival, Silvermine Guild Arts Center, 1037 Silvermine Rd., New Canaan; (203) 966-5618 (programs); www.silver mineart.org. Evening concerts.

SEPTEMBER
Annual Fairfield County Region Antique Car Show, East Ridge Middle School, Ridgefield. An annual event, held the first Sat after Labor Day from 10 a.m. to 3 p.m. The longest-running antique car show in America. It is the last pre-World War II antique car show in America, which means entries are restricted to unmodified 1942-and-older vehicles. The show usually draws more than 200 cars. Contact the Horseless Carriage Club of America (www.hcca .org) for more information.

Other Recommended Restaurants and Lodgings . . . .

NEW CANAAN
Roger Sherman Inn, 195 Oenoke Ridge; (203) 966-4541; www .rogershermaninn.com. An antiques-furnished inn with just seven rooms, some with fireplaces.

Tequila Mockingbird, 6 Forest St. (between East Avenue and Locust); (203) 966-2222. A Mexican-style cafe with terracotta tiled floors, a gaily painted mural, and a good selection of South-western and Mexican dishes.

RIDGEFIELD

Bernard's Inn at Ridgefield, 20 West Lane; (203) 438-8282; www .bernardsridgefield.com. A small inn known for its French cuisine and its Victorian patio gardens.

Stonehenge Inn, Route 7; (203) 438-6511; www.stonehengeinn-ct .com. This is both a wonderful restaurant serving French cuisine and a country inn. Its photogenic pond and grounds are every bridal couple's dream backdrop.

West Lane Inn, 22 West Lane; (203) 438-7323. A sixteen-room early-1800s colonial home restored with luxurious comforts.

For More Information . . . .

Coastal Fairfield County Convention and Visitors Bureau, 297 West Ave., Norwalk, CT 06850; (203) 853-7770 or (800) 866-7925; www.coastalct.com.

Connecticut Tourism Division, 505 Hudson St., Hartford, CT 06106; (860) 270-8080 or (800) 282-6863; www.ctbound.org.

NEW ENGLAND ESCAPE *Three*
Lower Connecticut River Valley
RIVER VALLEY TOWNS / 1 NIGHT

River views

River history

Eighteenth- and 19th-century houses

Antiques shops

Traditional New England fare

Vintage steam train

Riverboat cruise

Art galleries

With its roots back in the settlement of the New World, this little piece of south-central Connecticut is densely historic. Back in the early 1600s, many Colonists settled along the banks of the Connecticut River, from which trading (with ports as far away as the West Indies and the Mediterranean) became a popular activity for centuries to follow.

Today the area is punctuated with small scenic towns that were originally established as shipbuilding and merchant communities. Along the way there are several worthwhile restaurants specializing in New England cuisine, shops where you can buy crafts, antiques, and artwork, and truly warm and welcoming inns.

This two-day excursion takes you to the highlights of the area, including Essex, which is one of Connecticut's most visited towns. Be advised that during summer weekends it can be uncomfortably crowded.

DAY 1 / MORNING

The quickest and most direct route to the area from Manhattan is I-95, which roughly follows the Connecticut shoreline. Get off at Westbrook (exit 65) and turn right onto Route 153. Follow Route

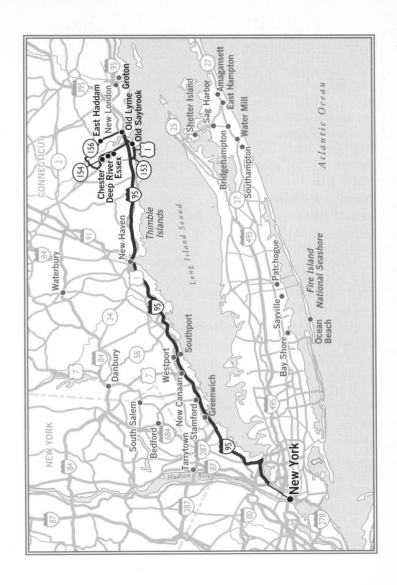

153 until you come to Route 1, which is locally known as the Shore Route, a road that takes you past picturesque marinas and salt marshes and into **Old Saybrook,** your first stop of the day.

Once a shipbuilding and fishing town, Old Saybrook is now a popular spot for summer vacationers. If you're traveling during a summer weekend, take time out to see the Georgian-style **General William Hart House,** 350 Main St. (860-388-2622; www.oldsay brook.com/attractions), which was once the residence of a prosperous merchant and politician. Home of the Old Saybrook Historical Society, it is open limited hours and by appointment; call ahead. Those in the market for antiques might want to check out **Essex Saybrook Antiques Village,** 345 Middlesex Turnpike (Route 154) (860-388-0689), where about 130 antiques dealers display their wares.

Afterward continue along Route 154 to head inland to **Essex,** which is home to a stunning collection of beautiful colonial and Federal houses that were built during the town's 18th-century shipbuilding days. The best way to enjoy Essex is to wander about on foot. Main Street is lined with shops selling sweets, jewelry, antiques, artwork, clothing—you name it. To see some of the town's oldest houses, walk up Pratt Street. One of the landmark buildings in town is the **Griswold Inn,** 36 Main St. (860-767-1776; www.griswoldinn.com), where you can settle in for lunch. Dating from 1776, this Essex institution is affectionately referred to as the Gris (pronounced "Griz"). To reach it, walk down Main Street (from Essex Square).

LUNCH The Griswold Inn is well known and respected for both its accommodations and its food. At lunchtime you can try its own brand of sausages or order a sandwich or salad plate.

AFTERNOON

From the Griswold Inn, walk to what is known as the Foot of Main, and you'll come to the **Connecticut River Museum,** 67 Main St., Steamboat Dock (860-767-8269; www.ctrivermuseum.org). It is housed in a restored 1878 warehouse where steamboats used to stop on their trips between New York and Hartford, unloading passengers and/or freight. A noteworthy attraction in the museum is a full-size reproduction of the American Turtle, the world's first submarine. Hours are 10 a.m. to 5 p.m. Tues through Sun.

From downtown Essex follow Route 154 (Railroad Avenue) west toward Ivoryton, and you'll come to the **Valley Railroad Station,** 1 Railroad Ave. (860-767-0103 or 800-377-9387; www.essexsteam train.com), where you can get tickets for the Essex Steam Train and Riverboat. The Steam Train hoots and whistles its way through the countryside to Chester and back, taking about an hour and a half. You can also combine the train ride with a riverboat sightseeing cruise by getting off at the Deep River station. The combination train/boat ride adds up to about three hours of your time. The main season for the Steam Train and Riverboat is May through Oct; call for information on their Christmas schedule.

Afterward you can continue upriver by following Route 154 (just keep bearing right when the road forks). It'll take you right to **Deep River,** your home for the night.

DINNER In nearby Ivoryton you'll find the **Copper Beech Inn,** 46 Main St. (860-767-0330 or 888-809-2056; www.copperbeechinn.com), for an elegant French meal. There are also thirteen rooms for staying overnight at this 1890 country home.

LODGING **Riverwind Country Inn,** 209 Main St. (860-526-2014; www .riverwindinn.com), has just eight rooms (all with private bath), each beautifully decorated with antiques and stenciling. There are also several common rooms with fireplaces.

DAY 2 / MORNING

BREAKFAST   A Southern buffet breakfast (ham, biscuits, hot casseroles, fresh fruit, coffee cake) is included in the room rate at the **Riverwind Country Inn.**

Return to Route 154 and follow it to **Chester,** an attractive village most writers cannot resist calling picture-postcard perfect. Indeed it is. Turn left from Route 154 onto Main Street and you'll find a handful of shops, galleries, and restaurants in the buildings that line the street. Also in Chester is the **Connecticut River Artisans Cooperative,** 5 West Main St. (800-526-5575; www.ctartisans.com), which showcases one-of-a-kind works including paintings, photographs, furniture, pottery, folk art, jewelry, and clothing. Call for hours.

Just east of the town center, on Route 148, you can climb aboard a ferry that's been shuttling between the east and west banks of the Connecticut River since 1769. The five-minute crossing operates throughout the day, from Apr through Nov, at a nominal charge.

Once onboard, all eyes turn to **Gillette Castle State Park,** 67 River Rd., East Haddam (860-526-2336), which looms over the river on the east bank in East Haddam. It was built as a dreamhouse-come-to-life by the actor/playwright William Gillette. When he died, the state of Connecticut purchased it and turned it and the surrounding land into a state park. There are picnic grounds, restrooms, food concession stands, and canoe rentals. Call for more information. The castle is open from Memorial Day through Columbus Day, daily from 10 a.m. to 4:30 p.m. There are limited hours also in Oct and Nov (call ahead).

Also in **East Haddam,** you'll find the **Goodspeed Opera House,** Route 82 (860-873-8668; www.goodspeed.org), which has a state-wide (and actually, even wider) reputation for reviving old American musicals. The opera house itself, a Victorian jewel, is exquisite both inside and out. Tours are given on Mon and Sat in July, Aug, and Sept. The theater season runs from Apr to Dec.

East Haddam is an attraction in itself, with many impeccably preserved buildings dating from the steamboat days. There's also a little red schoolhouse where Nathan Hale taught from 1773 to 1774, before he was hanged as a spy by the British.

LUNCH Across from Goodspeed, you'll find **La Vita Gustosa,** 9 Main St. (860-873-8999; www.lavitagustosa.com), a family-owned Italian trattoria. Be sure to make reservations, especially if there's a matinee at the theater that day.

Head south on Route 156 to **Old Lyme,** which is right near the mouth of the river, across from Old Saybrook. Its popularity began in the days of clipper ships and the China trade but later, like all beautiful places, it was discovered and colonized by quite a few artists, including Childe Hassam, Willard Metcalf, and Henry Ward Ranger, who called themselves American Impressionists. These artists stayed at "Miss Florence's" boardinghouse, which is now the **Florence Griswold Museum,** 96 Lyme St. (860-434-5542; www.flogris.org). Florence Griswold, an art lover, was the daughter of a ship captain. The house, which was built in 1817, is filled with period furnishings and showcases changing exhibitions that include New England furnishings and decorative arts. The main gallery houses an expansive collection of American art donated to the museum by the Hartford Steam Boiler Inspection and Insurance Company. It's open from Apr through Dec, Tues through Sat from 10 a.m. to 5 p.m. and Sun from 1 to 5 p.m. The rest of the year, it's open Tues through Sun from 1 to 5 p.m.

Other worthwhile stops in town include the **First Congregational Church** on Lyme Street (860-434-0220), which is a 1910 copy of the original 1816 structure that was destroyed by fire, and the **Lyme Academy of Fine Arts,** 84 Lyme St. (860-434-5232; www .lymeacademy.edu), which has changing exhibits during the summer months. Hours are Tues through Sat from 10 a.m. to 4 p.m. and Sun from 1 to 4 p.m. The Lyme Art Association (90 Lyme St.; 860-434-7802; www.lymeart.com) was founded in 1914. It presents rotating exhibits of the work of local and national artists.

From Old Lyme you can easily hop back on I-95 south and return to New York City.

There's More . . . .

Cruises. **Camelot Cruises,** 1 Marine Park, Haddam (860-345-8591; www.camelotcruises.com), offers lunch, dinner, Sunday brunch, and special-theme cruises (mystery outings, fall foliage trips) aboard the 400-passenger cruise ship Camelot.

Parks. **The Selden Neck State Park** is a 528-acre park in the Connecticut River that you can reach only by water. It's located 2 miles south of **Gillette Castle State Park** in East Haddam, from which you can get additional information and permits (call 860-526-2336). Canoes and kayaks can be launched at the ferry slip below the castle. **Hammonasset Beach State Park,** Route 1, Madison (860-245-2785), is the largest of Connecticut's shoreline parks. Visit www.dep.state.ct.us/stateparks.

Thimble Islands. If you have extra time as you're heading towards Old Saybrook on I-95, consider detouring at exit 56 to take a narrated cruise of the Thimble Islands. This little archipelago is made up of dozens of small rocky islands that are a nesting stop for migrating seals. The tours run May through Oct (weather permitting), leaving from the Stony Creek town dock. There are a couple of cruise companies including **Captain Bob's** (www.thimbleislands .com), **Thimble Island Cruise** (www.thimbleislandcruise.com) and **Captain Dave's Thimble Island Cruises** (www.thimbleislander.com) offering a selection of tour lengths and departure times.

Special Events . . . .

FEBRUARY
Annual Winter Carnivale and Ice Competition in Chester Center. This very popular event attracts ice carvers—both amateur and professional—and includes a variety of events, including the Chilly Chili Cook-Off.

JULY
Annual Ancient Muster, Deep River. Fifty to seventy fife-and-drum corps recall Revolutionary War days in this annual parade that has been taking place for more than 120 years.

Annual Arts and Crafts Show, Old Saybrook. Held on the Town Green and Main Street, this annual event attracts more than 25,000 people.

DECEMBER
Torchlight Parade, Old Saybrook. This parade is a tradition that dates from early colonial days. Fife-and-drum corps march down Main Street to meet townspeople on the Town Green to sing carols.

Victorian Christmas at Gillette Castle in East Haddam. Every year the castle is decorated with evergreens and Victorian ornaments. Musical groups perform on weekend afternoons; (860) 526-2336.

Other Recommended Restaurants and Lodgings . . . .

EAST HADDAM

Bishopsgate Inn, 7 Norwich Rd.; (860) 873-1677; www.bishops gate.com. Right across from the Goodspeed Opera House, this early-19th-century shipbuilder's house has half a dozen tastefully decorated rooms, all with theatrical names.

ESSEX

Griswold Inn, 36 Main St.; (860) 767-1776; www.griswoldinn.com. In addition to dining (described earlier in this chapter), "the Gris" is a fine choice for staying overnight. It's every inch New England, with exposed rough-hewn rafters, low ceilings, and hooked rugs. Its Sun morning "Hunt Breakfasts" are legendary, with help-yourself, unlimited servings of all sorts of breakfast favorites, including kippers and grits.

OLD LYME

The Chestnut Grille at The Bee and Thistle Inn, 100 Lyme St. (860-434-1667 or 800-622-4946; www.beeandthistleinn.com) serves dinner Wed through Sat nights. Consider going on a Wed or Thurs, when they offer a prix fixe meal ($28) that includes their chocolate chestnut bourbon torte with sweet bourbon cream.

Old Lyme Inn, 85 Lyme St.; (860) 434-2600; www.oldlymeinn .com. Dating from the 1850s, this clapboard farmhouse is beautifully furnished with canopy beds, marble-topped dressers, and antique pieces. The dining room is open for lunch and dinner.

OLD SAYBROOK

Saybrook Point Inn and Spa, 2 Bridge St.; (860) 395-2000 or (800) 243-0212; www.saybrook.com. An eighty-room contemporary hotel with 18th-century repro English decor. Ask for a room facing the marina.

WESTBROOK
Water's Edge Resort & Spa, 1525 Boston Post Rd.; (860) 399-5901; www.watersedge-resort.com. This is a full-service resort set on a bluff overlooking Long Island Sound. It sprawls over fifteen acres and has an impressive spa.

For More Information . . . .

Connecticut Tourism Division, 505 Hudson St., Hartford, CT 06106; (860) 270-8080 or (800) 282-6863; www.ctbound.org.

NEW ENGLAND ESCAPE *Four*
Southeastern Shoreline
MARITIME MYSTIC AND MORE / 1 NIGHT

Historic ships
Submarines
Sea and river ports
Maritime museum
Shopping
Seafood dining
Aquarium

Connecticut's maritime roots are most visible in this part of the state, especially in the towns of New London, Groton, Mystic, and Stonington.

You could easily spend a whole day at Mystic Seaport; however, there are many other attractions in the area. Consider combining this trip with the Southern New England Escape Three, which takes you to the nearby towns in the Lower Connecticut River Valley.

DAY 1 / MORNING

Like the rest of the Connecticut shoreline, this area can be easily reached by taking I-95 north. Set out as early as you can, as there is a lot to squeeze into two days.

Make your first stop **New London** (exit 83), a former whaling town. The number-one attraction here is the **United States Coast Guard Academy,** 15 Mohegan Ave. (860-444-8444; www.cga.edu). Visitors can tour the grounds, the visitor center and museum, the chapel, and the tall ship Eagle when it's in port. The latter is used by cadets for training purposes.

Whale Oil Row, 105–119 Huntington St., is another interesting attraction in New London. It's a collection of four 1832 temple-front mansions.

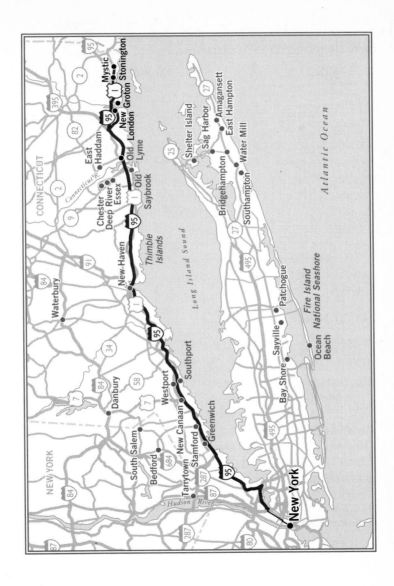

Also in town is the **Monte Cristo Cottage,** 325 Pequot Ave. (860-443-0051; www.oneilltheatercenter.org), which was the boyhood home of playwright Eugene O'Neill as well as the setting for two of his plays, *Ah! Wilderness* and *Long Day's Journey into Night.*

From New London it's a short drive east to **Groton,** which is known as "The Submarine Capital of the World." Indeed, this shore-hugging community is home to the **USS *Nautilus* Memorial,** U.S. Naval Base, One Crystal Lake Rd. (800-343-0079; www.ussnautilus.org). The USS *Nautilus* was the world's first nuclear-powered submarine and is now a National Historic Landmark, permanently berthed. There are meticulously assembled museum displays recounting the history of the U.S. Submarine Force. It's open for touring year-round, but hours vary; call ahead.

From Groton drive east on Route 1 to **Mystic,** where you'll find the famed **Mystic Seaport,** 50 Greenmanville Ave. (860-572-5315 or 888-973-2767; www.visitmysticseaport.com), a huge open-air museum. It's open daily, year-round, except Christmas Day. Admission prices vary. Shops and exhibits are open from 9 a.m. to 5 p.m. Apr through Oct, and 10 a.m. to 4 p.m. Nov through Mar. Start by taking time out for lunch.

LUNCH   **The Seamen's Inne,** 75 Greenmanville Ave. (860-572-5303; www.seamensinne.org), is located right next to the seaport entrance. A Connecticut landmark, it serves New England fare and is well known for its fresh fish and prime rib.

AFTERNOON

Once you've fortified yourself with a good lunch, head into the Mystic Seaport. Here you'll see more historic seagoing vessels—from

a dugout canoe to America's sole surviving wooden whaling ship—
than most people see in a lifetime. The star attraction for many is
the 113-foot *Charles W. Morgan,* a whaling ship that was built in
1841. The height of America's shipbuilding and whaling prosper-
ity is magnificently captured at this seventeen-acre living-history
museum. On land there are dozens of 19th-century buildings that
were brought to the seaport and restored. Highly skilled men and
women, in period costume, demonstrate various maritime skills
such as sail handling, oystering, and ropework. Allow at least a
couple of hours (even three or four) to roam around.

Shoppers shouldn't miss the **Mystic Seaport Museum Store**
(www.visitmysticseaport.com), which is right at the main gate
(South Gate). There are two floors where you can find all sorts of
must-haves, from simple old-fashioned candies to multi-thousand
dollar lightship baskets. It's open daily from 10 a.m. to 5:30 p.m.
You'll find more shops inside the seaport, but this one gets first
prize.

DINNER **Abbott's Lobster in the Rough,** 117 Pearl St., Noank (860-
536-7719; www.abbotts-lobster.com), is a must if you love seafood. It's a huge,
massively popular seaside restaurant with picnic tables upon which huge platters
of spanking-fresh seafood are devoured. Expect to wait in line. Noank is about ten
minutes south of Mystic. The restaurant is closed during the winter.

LODGING **The Old Mystic Inn,** 52 Main St., Old Mystic (860-572-9422;
www.oldmysticinn.com). Not to be confused with the Inn at Mystic, this eight-room
inn is in nearby Old Mystic (1½ miles north of I-95 on Route 27), which makes it
within easy reach of the seaport and all the other area attractions but sets it apart
from the crowd. The building, which was built in the early 1800s, was originally the
Old Mystic Book Shop.

DAY 2 / MORNING

....

BREAKFAST   A country breakfast (coffee, tea, or hot chocolate, plus juice and pancakes or French toast or eggs, any style) is included in the room rate at the **Old Mystic Inn.**

After breakfast take a look around the **Mystic Aquarium,** 55 Coogan Blvd. (860-572-5955; www.mysticaquarium.org), which is home to all sorts of amphibians and other marine habitants, including sea lions, seals, and penguins. The aquarium is open daily from 9 a.m. to 6 p.m. from July through Labor Day. All other times the daily hours are 9 a.m. to 5 p.m.

If you feel like doing a little shopping, head for **Olde Mystick Village** (entrances are on Coogan Boulevard; 860-536-4941). The village is a collection of colonial-style buildings housing about sixty shops that sell an assortment of souvenirs, local food products, and other items.

From Olde Mystick Village drive east on Route 1 for about 5 miles, and you'll come to **Stonington,** a traditional New England seacoast village that deserves a walk around. To get the lay of the land, start by climbing the stone steps to the top of the tower at the **Old Lighthouse Museum,** 7 Water St. (860-535-1440). Inside the 1823 granite lighthouse, there are displays of maritime history and memorabilia of the Orient trade and whaling and fishing days. It's open from May through Oct, but hours vary, so call ahead. Then wander about admiring the 18th- and 19th-century architecture throughout the town. Water Street is the town's main street, where you'll find several boutiques, antiques shops, and restaurants.

LUNCH The pizza is quite good at **Mystic Pizza,** 56 West Main St.; (860) 536-3700; www.mysticpizza.com, the pizza restaurant that Julia Roberts made famous in the movie of the same name.

AFTERNOON

After lunch head back to New York on I-95.

There's More . . . .

Beach and amusement complex. **Ocean Beach Park,** near Harkness Memorial State Park south of New London, exit 75–76 from I-95; (860) 447-3031; www.ocean-beach-park.com. This major recreation area has saltwater and pool swimming, nature trails, and amusement rides.

Casinos. **Foxwoods Resort Casino** on Route 2 in **Mashantucket** (800-752-9244; www.foxwoods.com) and the **Mohegan Sun Casino** in Uncasville (888-226-7711; www.mohegansun.com) attract thousands of visitors daily. Both are open daily, 24 hours a day.

Hiking. There are more than twenty parks with trails for all levels of hikers throughout the Mystic Coast and County region.

Museums. The **Children's Museum of Southeastern Connecticut** (409 Main St., Niantic; 860-691-1111; www.childrensmuseum sect.org) is a hands-on interactive museum for children ages 1 through 12. The **Mashantucket Pequot Museum and Research Center** (110 Pequot Trail, Mashantucket; 800-411-9671; www.mash antucket.com) has extensive permanent exhibits on the native and natural history of New England.

Spa. In nearby **Norwich** the **Norwich Inn & Spa,** 607 West Thames St.; (860) 886-2401 or (800) 275-4772; www.thespaatnorwich inn.com. Facilities include a full-service health spa.

Theater. **Eugene O'Neill Theater Center,** 305 Great Neck Rd., Waterford; (860) 443-5378; www.oneilltheatercenter.org. An organization devoted to developing new stage works.

Special Events . . . .

MAY
Lobster Weekend, Mystic Seaport, Mystic. Lobster feasts, music, and other entertainment, www.visitmysticseaport.com.

JUNE
Yale–Harvard Regatta, New London. A rowing regatta with crews from both Yale and Harvard universities.

FOURTH OF JULY
Independence Weekend, Mystic. A re-creation of an 1870s Fourth of July by costumed role-players. Also a parade and other activities, www.mycoast.com.

OCTOBER
Chowderfest Weekend. Every year Mystic Seaport hosts its annual battle of the chowderpots, where local community groups serve up their own versions of the perfect chowder. The festival includes folk music, gallery exhibitions, and all sorts of activities, www.visit mysticseaport.com.

Other Recommended Restaurants and Lodging

MASHANTUCKET

Grand Pequot Tower at Foxwoods, Route 2; (800) 369-9663; www .foxwoods.com. A world-class hotel with 824 rooms and suites, gourmet restaurants, and casinos.

MYSTIC

Captain Daniel Packer Inne, 32 Water St.; (860) 536-3555; www .danielpacker.com. A 250-year-old restaurant serving American fare, including rack of spring lamb, filet mignon, and some fish dishes.

Inn at Mystic, on US 1, at junction of Route 27 (2 miles south of I-95, exit 90); (860) 536-9604; www.innatmystic.com. A sixty-seven-room inn one-quarter mile from Long Island Sound; some rooms have fireplaces, some have whirlpools.

Steamboat Inn, 73 Steamboat Wharf; (860) 536-8300; www .steamboatinnmystic.com. Located in the heart of Mystic, right on the river. Six of the rooms have fireplaces; four have kitchenettes.

NIANTIC

Fourteen Lincoln Street, 14 Lincoln St.; (860) 739-6327; www .14lincolnstreet.com. This is a very small and tasteful inn just 2 blocks from the beach. There are just four rooms, each with its own private bath and hot tub. Check the Web site for the gourmet retreats they offer.

NORTH STONINGTON
Another Second Penny Inn, 870 Pequot Trail; (860) 535-1710; www.secondpenny.com. This 1710 colonial home offers two large guest rooms and one suite. It sits on almost five acres of gardens, fields, and forests 3 miles from downtown Mystic.

Randall's Ordinary, Route 2; (860) 599-4540. An eighteen-room colonial wayside inn listed on the National Register of Historic Places and also listed on the Connecticut Freedom Trail. Authentic colonial cuisine prepared entirely in an open-hearth fireplace.

For More Information . . . .

Connecticut Tourism Division, 505 Hudson St., Hartford, CT 06106; (860) 270-3405 or (800) 282-6863; www.ctbound.org.

Mystic Coast and County Travel Industry Association, 101 Water St., Norwich, CT 06360; (860) 204-0310; www.mycoast.com.

NEW ENGLAND ESCAPE *Five*

Northeast Corner
A QUIET GETAWAY / 1 NIGHT

The nickname for the northeastern corner of Connecticut is "The Quiet Corner." Indeed it is quiet. It's also one of the Northeast's most unspoiled chunks of land, made up of fertile pastures, low-rising hills, rivers, forests, and historic villages.

> Farms
> Historic homes
> Mill villages
> Scenic highway
> Bird-watching
> Antiquing
> University of Connecticut

DAY 1 / MORNING

To reach the area, take I-684 north to I-84 east. Get off at exit 67 and go south on Route 31 to the junction of Route 44. Take 44 east to Route 31 again and follow that into **Coventry,** where you'll find **Caprilands Herb Farm,** 534 Silver St. (860-742-7244). The farm, which has an 18th-century farmhouse, was owned by author and herbalist Adelma Simmons, who died in 1997. Spend some time walking through the herb gardens, check out the shops, and then sip a cup of herbal tea in the dining room. It's open daily; garden tours are conducted by request.

Coventry has a handful of other attractions, including the **Nathan Hale Homestead,** 2299 South St. (860-742-6917; www .thebirdinhand.com/nhale.htm), which was the family home of the state hero. It's open from May 15 through Oct 15, from 1 to 4 p.m. Wed through Sun. Nearby is the **Strong–Porter House Museum,** 2382 South St. (860-742-7847), a farmhouse that was built around 1730 by a great-uncle of Nathan Hale. There are several

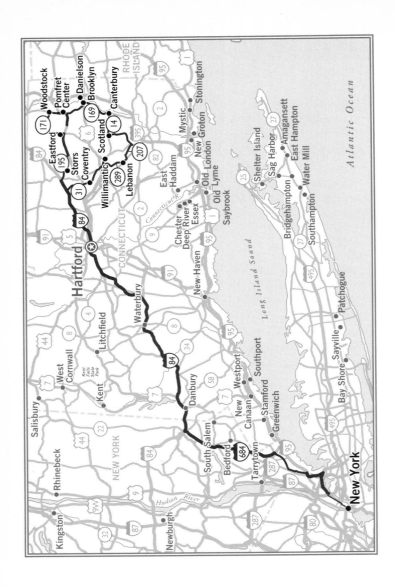

outbuildings to tour, including a carpenter's shop, a carriage shed, and a barn with exhibits. You can buy a combined ticket for admission to both this museum and the Nathan Hale Homestead. In Coventry there's also an old one-room schoolhouse called the **Brick School House,** Merrow Road (860-742-1419), which was built between 1823 and 1825. It's open by appointment only.

LUNCH   **Bidwell Tavern,** 1260 Main St. (860-742-6978; www .bidwelltavern.com), is located right in the heart of Coventry's antiquing district. It's a historic restaurant serving New England cuisine, including a wonderful Yankee pot roast.

AFTERNOON

From Coventry drive a short distance south to **Willimantic,** where you can stop to see the **Windham Textile and History Museum,** 157 Union and Main Street (860-456-2178; www.millmuseum.org). It's a fascinating museum, with exhibits devoted to textile production at the height of the Industrial Revolution. There's a re-created 1880s mill shop floor, a company store, a tenement home, a library dating from 1877, and a mill agent's mansion. Hours vary; call ahead.

Make your next stop in the town of **Lebanon** (follow Route 289 south). There are some very worthwhile attractions here, including the **Jonathan Trumbull Jr. House,** 780 Trumbull Hwy., on the Green (860-642-6100; www.jtrumbulljr.org), and the Trumbull family's store, which is known as the **Revolutionary War Office,** 149 West Town St. (860-873-3399). Trumbull was the only colonial governor who supported America's war for independence. The war office stocked war supplies and became a meeting place of the Council of Safety. Also on West Town Street is the **Dr. William Beaumont House,** 169 West Town St., on the Green (860-642-7247). This

18th-century cottage was the birthplace of the "Father of Physiology of Digestion." Inside there are several displays of early surgical instruments. All three have very limited hours, so call ahead.

From Lebanon head east on Route 207 and turn left onto Route 97. Then turn right on Route 14 East. That will take you right into **Canterbury,** where you'll find the **Prudence Crandall House Museum,** at the junction of Routes 14 and 169 (860-546-9916). This was New England's first school for black women. It's open Wed through Sun from 10 a.m. to 4:30 p.m.; closed mid-Dec through the end of Mar. Canterbury is also home to **Wright's Mill Tree Farm,** 63 Creasey Rd. (860-774-1455; www.wrightsmillfarm.com), which has more than 250 acres of ponds, waterfalls, and mill sites to explore. It's open daily from 9 a.m. to 5 p.m. year-round.

Turn left onto Route 169 and you'll find yourself passing through a densely scenic landscape. This road has been designated by Scenic America as one of the ten most scenic highways in the United States.

Continue about 7 miles to **Brooklyn** and stop to have a look around the **Daniel Putnam Tyler Law Office,** on Route 169 (860-774-7728), where Tyler practiced law from 1822 to 1875. Hours are very limited, however, so call ahead. Brooklyn is home to the **New England Center for Contemporary Art,** 7 Putnam Place (860-774-8899; www.museum-necca.org), which showcases changing exhibits in its pre-Revolutionary barn setting. It's open Wed through Sun from 1 to 5 p.m. from Apr through Nov. Brooklyn also has two beautiful churches to see: the **Unitarian Church** on the Green and **Old Trinity Church** (take Route 6 east for a mile and turn left onto Church Street). Both date from 1771. In nearby Danielson (follow Route 6 east of town), you'll find **Logee's Greenhouses,** 141 North St. (860-774-8038; www.logees.com), which has more than 2,000 varieties of indoor plants, including 400 types of begonias. The greenhouses are open Mon through Sat from 9 a.m. to 5 p.m.

and Sun from 11 a.m. to 5 p.m. (You'll be coming back to Brooklyn for dinner.)

Continue north to the picturesque town of **Pomfret Center,** which is home to the elite Pomfret Preparatory School. You can tour the village's last mill, which is now a museum listed on the National Register of Historic Places known as the **Brayton Grist Mill,** Route 44 (entrance is at Mashamoquet Brook State Park). Pomfret Center is also home to the **Connecticut Audubon Center** at Pomfret, 189 Pomfret St. (860-928-4948; www.ctaudubon.org). You'll find some of the best birding in the state of Connecticut on its 667 acres.

Woodstock, about 5 miles from Pomfret Center, is next on your itinerary as well as your stopover for the night. Try to get there before 5 p.m. so that you can get in to see **Roseland Cottage–Bowen House,** 556 Route 169 (860-928-4074). Roseland is a Gothic Revival summerhouse that was built by merchant and publisher Henry Bowen. Be sure to take a look inside the barn; it contains what's possibly the oldest indoor bowling alley in the country. The cottage, which is filled with original family furnishings, is open from June 1 through Oct 15, Fri through Sun. Tours given every hour from 11 a.m. to 4 p.m.

DINNER **The Golden Lamb Buttery,** 499 Wolf Den Rd., Brooklyn (860-774-4423; www.thegoldenlamb.com), is located in a converted barn well known among gourmets. The menu generally includes classic American dishes and whatever's ready to be plucked from the garden. There's usually a wonderful soup to start, followed by a choice of entrees (duck, lamb, various seafood) prepared a different way every day. Advance reservations are a must.

LODGING **The Inn at Woodstock Hill,** 94 Plaine Hill Rd. (off Route 169) (860-928-0528; www.woodstockhill.com), is a twenty-two-room inn listed on the National Register of Historic Places. It's a restored country estate on nineteen rolling acres.

DAY 2 / MORNING

BREAKFAST　　A continental breakfast (included in the room rate) is served at the **Inn at Woodstock Hill.**

If you're interested in antiquing, head east on Route 171 to **Putnam,** which has several antiques shops. Then head west on Route 44, which will take you to **Storrs,** the area's cultural center. You could stay busy for hours browsing through the collections at the **University of Connecticut** alone: the Atrium Gallery of Contemporary Art (860-486-3930); the William Benton Museum of Art, which features European and American works (860-486-4520); and the Connecticut State Museum of Natural History (860-486-4460). For more information, visit www.uconn.edu. By the way, "UConn" has a dairy bar where the ice cream is nonpareil. It's just off Route 195 in Storrs. All the ice cream is homemade. It's a more than fifty-year-old UConn tradition.

Non-university attractions nearby include the **Gurleyville Grist Mill,** Stone Mill Road, Mansfield (860-429-9023), which is the state's only remaining stone gristmill. Hours are limited; call ahead. The **Mansfield Historical Society Museum,** 954 Storrs Rd., Storrs (860-429-6575), has exhibits relating to local history. Hours are limited; call ahead.

LUNCH　　**Angellino's Restaurant,** 135–A Storrs Rd., Mansfield (860-450-7071; www.angellinos.com), serves Italian food. Be sure to try the penne Augino—with artichoke hearts, sun-dried tomatoes, and garlic.

AFTERNOON

Return to New York City by heading north on Route 195 to I-84 west. Take I-84 right over the New York border and head south on I-684.

There's More . . . .

Auto racing. Due north of Storrs, in Stafford Springs, is the **Stafford Motor Speedway,** Route 140; (860) 684-2783; www.staffordmotor speedway.com.

Special Events . . . .

MID-MAY
Springtime Festival, Danielson. A parade, a road race, arts and crafts, food booths, a petting zoo, and more.

SEPTEMBER
Woodstock Fair, on the fairgrounds at Routes 169 and 171, South Woodstock. This is the state's best-attended family fair. There's a horse show, go-kart racing, vaudeville acts, arts and crafts—you name it.

Lions Outdoor Arts and Crafts Show, Davis Park, Danielson. More than 150 artists and artisans from all over the Northeast show their work here.

OCTOBER
Oktoberfest, Wright's Mill Farm, 63 Creasey Rd., Canterbury; (860) 774-1455; www.wrightsmillfarm.com. Includes full German buffet and yodeling contest.

Other Recommended Restaurants and Lodgings . . . .

POMFRET
Celebrations Inn, 330 Pomfret St.; (860) 928-5492 or (877) 928-5492; www.celebrationsinn.com. A wonderful place to relax and

enjoy Connecticut's "Quiet Corner," Celebrations Inn is an 1885 Queen Anne Victorian, which the innkeepers have billed "festive." All of the rooms are beautifully furnished with antiques.

The Harvest Restaurant, 37 Putnam Rd.; (860) 928-0008; www .harvestrestaurant.com. Especially noteworthy at this restaurant is the Sunday brunch, where you can sample truly original dishes such as the vanilla crème brûlée French toast, potato-leek pancakes, and a to-die-for seafood crepe.

STORRS
Altnaveigh Inn & Restaurant, Route 195; (860) 429-4490; www .altnaveighinn.com. This is a bed-and-breakfast in a farmhouse that was built in 1734. It has five rooms very simply decorated in a New England country style. Downstairs the restaurant serves seafood, beef, and chicken dishes. A continental breakfast is included in the room rate.

For More Information . . . .

Connecticut Tourism Division, 505 Hudson St., Hartford, CT 06106; (860) 270-8080 or (800) 282-6863; www.ctbound.org.

Northeast Connecticut Visitors District, 13 Canterbury Rd., Canterbury, CT 06331; (888) 628-1228; www.ctquietcorner.org.

NEW ENGLAND ESCAPE *Six*
The Litchfield Hills
TRADITIONAL NEW ENGLAND / 2 NIGHTS

For lots of wealthy New Yorkers and celebrities (Meryl Streep, Dustin Hoffman, and Henry Kissinger, to name just a few), this little northwestern corner of Connecticut is a "have your cake and eat it too" location. It has all the things that make New England New England, such as white steepled churches, stately old houses, covered bridges, stone walls, fields filled with large-eyed cows, and big old barns sagging with the contour of the land. At the same time the area is home to a surprising number of up-to-urban-standards restaurants (many with European- or Culinary Institute of America-trained chefs), dozens of art galleries and museums, and an impressive collection of inns and other buildings listed on the National Register of Historic Places.

New England scenery
Covered bridges
Antiques shops
Historic district
Woodland walks
Museums
Vineyards

There are more than three dozen towns scattered throughout the **Litchfield Hills,** most of them with fewer than 5,000 inhabitants. This short trip takes you to the area's highlights, on a loop tour that roughly begins and ends in New Milford.

DAY 1 / MORNING

Less than two hours from Manhattan (about 100 miles), the Litchfield area can be reached by following the Henry Hudson Parkway to the Saw Mill River Parkway to I-684 to I-84 east, then following

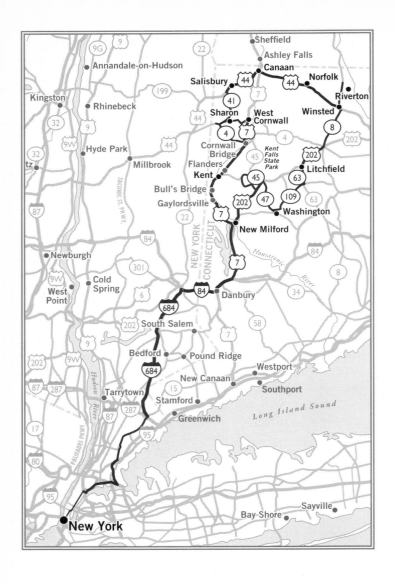

Route 7 north (exit 7) to **New Milford.** (An alternative route is to take I-684 north to Route 22 and cross over the state line on Route 55, heading into Gaylordsville.)

Either way, as you proceed north, you can't help feeling as though you've left the city far behind. Once you pass New Milford, it's time for passengers to stop reading the map or catnapping and start looking at the scenery. From here on the landscape is steadily scenic—wooded hills, vintage farmhouses, lakes and rivers that really do sparkle, and small villages that inevitably elicit all sorts of cliché adjectives like "charming," "postcard-perfect," and "cute."

If you're a food lover, consider making a stop at the **Silo: The Store and the School,** 44 Upland Rd. (860-355-0300; www.thesilo.com). This former farm is now a cooking school and retail store, with kitchenware from around the United States, Mexico, and Europe. Take a look around the adjoining silo, which usually has marked-down items for sale. Upstairs in the silo there's a gallery showcasing the work of local artists and artisans. On Suns there are often recitals accompanied by wine-and-cheese receptions. Call ahead for a schedule of events and, if you're interested in taking a class (on bread baking, low-fat Chinese, even barbecue cuisine), class schedules. All classes, which start in early spring and go on every weekend up to Christmas, are three hours long and self-contained.

Make your next stop **Bull's Bridge,** one of the state's two covered bridges that you can drive through (the other one is in nearby West Cornwall). It's just before Kent and spans the Housatonic River. As well as being very picturesque, the bridge has a historical claim to fame in that Washington crossed it back in 1781. Supposedly one of his horses fell in the river (it was March) and had to be pulled out.

Plan to spend a chunk of time in **Kent** (Route 7 takes you right through the heart of it), especially if you enjoy browsing around galleries and antiques shops. Be forewarned, however: Kent can be a mob scene on fall weekends.

Kent is also home to the **Sloane–Stanley Museum,** Route 7, about 2 miles north of Kent Center (860-566-3005; www.chc .state.ct.us/sloanestanleymuseum.htm), which has a collection of early American farm and woodworking tools that were amassed by Eric Sloane, the artist and writer. The museum is open from mid-May through Oct, Wed through Sun. Carry on and you'll come to **Flanders Historic District,** which is a preserved group of houses that were originally part of the center of Kent. One of them, the Seven Hearths, is now a museum filled with artwork by the American portrait painter George Lawrence Nelson.

A bit farther north on Route 7 is **Kent Falls State Park** (860-927-3238), a 295-acre park with a beautiful waterfall that's been featured in many ads. With its web of trails and picnic facilities, this is a lovely park in which to while away a couple of hours. You can climb up to the head of the falls (something like 25 feet) on a wide, stepped pathway.

LUNCH   **Fife 'n Drum Restaurant and Inn,** Route 7 (860-927-3509; www.fifendrum.com). A family-owned restaurant, this popular spot serves continental cuisine.

AFTERNOON

Continue north on Route 7 to **West Cornwall,** which many people consider Connecticut's prettiest town, where, on Route 128, you'll find the state's other passable **covered bridge.** It has been in continuous service since 1837. Detour a bit to **Sharon,** west on Route 4 or Route 128, if you'd like to see more beautiful New England scenery and pick your own fruit (strawberries in June and July, raspberries in July and Aug, and apples in Sept and Oct) at **Ellsworth Hill Farm** on Route 4 (860-364-0025; www.ellsworthfarm .com). Then stop at the **Audubon Center at Sharon,** 325 Route 4 (860-364-0520; www.audubon.org), a 2,000-acre sanctuary with self-guiding trails, wildflower and herb gardens, a farm area, an interpretive center, and a gift shop. It's open year-round, Mon through Sat from 9 a.m. to 5 p.m. and Sun from 1 to 5 p.m.

From Sharon head north on Route 41 to get to **Salisbury,** which is home to a handful of shops and a welcoming little tearoom called **Chaiwalla,** 1 Main St. (860-435-9758). There are more than a dozen teas imported from around the world, and each one is freshly brewed from Salisbury spring water. Of course, a cup of tea would not be complete on its own, so there is an equally impressive selection of edibles, including traditional scones, sausage pies, onion tarts, and a variety of desserts. Chaiwalla is open from 10 a.m. to 6 p.m. daily, year-round. Chaiwalla is also a center for tea tastings, lectures on tea, and poetry and short-story readings over tea.

In nearby **Lakeville** on Route 112, you'll find **Lime Rock Park,** where sports-car races take place from Apr through Nov. For ticket information call (860) 435-5000 or (800) 722-3577; www.lime rock.com.

From Salisbury it's a short drive up Route 44 to **Canaan,** which is home to the **Housatonic Railroad,** one of the nation's oldest railroads. There are scenic rides throughout the summer and autumn months. For details, call (860) 824-0850; www.housatonicrr.com.

Continue east on Route 44 to **Norfolk.** In the late 1800s Norfolk was a scheduled stop on the railroad between New York City and Pittsfield, Massachusetts. At that time it became a popular resort for the affluent, who built many of the large houses you see there today. The village green is surrounded by buildings that are listed on the National Register of Historic Places. There's a small historical museum at the **Norfolk Historical Society** here on the green (860-542-5761) that houses local artifacts and some old Connecticut-made clocks. It's open from mid-June through mid-Oct on Sat and Sun only. One of the most enjoyable ways to see the town is to take a **horse-drawn carriage** (or sleigh, in winter). For schedules, stop by or call **Loon Meadow Farm,** 41 Loon Meadow Dr. (860-542-6085; www.loonmeadowfarm.com).

Nearby there are a couple of hiking opportunities, including **Haystack Mountain,** 1 mile north on Route 272. From the top there are stunning views of the Berkshires and **Campbell Falls,** 6 miles north of Norfolk on Route 272. Two miles south of Norfolk, on Route 272, is **Dennis Hill,** which is topped by a summit pavilion (it used to be a summer residence) where you can get a far-reaching view of the Litchfield Hills.

DINNER **White Hart Inn,** Village Green (Routes 41 and 44), Salisbury (860-435-0030; www.whitehartinn.com). Whether you order the roast Chilean sea bass, the penne puttanesca, or the grilled pork chop, you will be satiated here. The dining rooms are located in the inn, which began operating in the 19th century and has since been meticulously renovated.

LODGING In Norfolk, the **Manor House,** 69 Maple Ave. (860-542-5690; www.manorhouse-norfolk.com), is an English Tudor mansion filled with antiques, with Tiffany stained-glass windows. All nine guest rooms have private bathrooms.

DAY 2 / MORNING

BREAKFAST At the **Manor House** bed-and-breakfast.

From Norfolk follow Route 44 east to **Winsted,** the self-proclaimed mountain-laurel capital, and then head north on Route 20 to **River-ton,** which has long been known as the "Laurel City" because of the abundance of laurel in the area. In fact, each year in June the town hosts the Laurel Festival, complete with a parade, the Laurel Ball, and the crowning of a Laurel Queen. In Winsted you can get on Route 8 and head south to Route 202 West, which will take you right to the town of **Litchfield.**

Litchfield is about as New England as a town can be, complete with a village green, a spick-and-span white church, and stately 18th-century houses lined up along wide maple-tree-lined streets as if contestants in a beauty pageant. The town, which sits on a plateau above the Naugatuck Valley, was spared early industrialization because the railroads laid their main lines down in the valley. Its most famous early resident was Harriet Beecher Stowe, author of Uncle Tom's Cabin. She grew up here.

One of Litchfield's most celebrated, and photographed, attractions is the **Congregational Church,** at the junction of Routes 202 and 118. Built in 1828, it's the perfect New England church. Also perfect is **Litchfield's green,** which was laid out in the 1770s. If time permits, have a look around the **Litchfield Historical Society Museum,** on the green, 7 South St. (860-567-4501; www.litchfieldhistoricalsociety.org), a good source of local history. It's open from mid-Apr through mid-Nov, Tues through Sat, from 11 a.m. to 5 p.m., and Sun from 1 to 5 p.m. The **Tapping Reeve House and Law School,** 82 South St. (860-567-4501; www.litchfieldct.com), are worth visiting. Both date from the 1700s. The law school was America's first and included graduates Aaron Burr and John C. Calhoun. They're open from mid-Apr through mid-Oct, Tues through Sat from 11 a.m. to 5 p.m., and Sun from 1 to 5 p.m.

Also in Litchfield, just off Route 118 on Chestnut Hill Road, is the **Haight Vineyard and Winery** (860-567-4045; www.haightvineyards.com), where tours and tastings take place year-round except on major holidays.

For those wanting to get a little fresh air, the **White Memorial Foundation** is a 4,000-acre conservation area 2½ miles west of town on Route 202 (860-567-0857; www.whitememorialcc .org). There are more than 35 miles of trails threaded through the woodlands.

Just south of town is **White Flower Farm,** Route 63 (860-567-8789; www.whiteflowerfarm.com), a sprawling retail and mail-order nursery with ten acres of display gardens and thirty acres of growing fields. The farm is open from 9 a.m. to 6 p.m. daily from Apr through Sept and 10 a.m. to 5 p.m. daily from Oct through Mar.

LUNCH **The West Street Grill,** 43 West St. (860-567-3885), is right in the center of town. Grab a table outside if the weather's nice and watch the passersby. Lunch dishes include great salads using lots of locally grown ingredients, as well as burgers, pastas, and some fish dishes.

AFTERNOON

From Litchfield head south on Route 63, then turn right onto Route 109, and follow that to **Washington,** a little village built around a church. There are a handful of sights to check out in the area, including the **Gunn Memorial Library and Museum,** on the green, 5 Wykeham Rd. (860-868-7756; www.gunnlibrary.org), a house built in 1781 containing local-history collections and exhibits, antique furniture, old dolls, and doll houses (call for hours), and the **Institute for American Indian Studies,** 38 Curtis Rd. (860-868-0518; www.birdstone.org), which houses an impressive collection of Indian artifacts as well as a complete outdoor Indian village. The latter is open from 10 a.m. to 5 p.m. Mon through Sat and noon to 5 p.m. Sun.

DINNER   The restaurant at the **Mayflower Inn,** 118 Woodbury Rd. (Route 47) (860-868-9466; www.mayflowerinn.com), is not only beautifully situated at one of the state's best inns but has wonderful food and wines to match.

LODGING   **The Mayflower Inn** has thirty rooms and suites, all overlooking gardens filled with rare flora. It also has a spa with yoga classes, "soul-revival rituals," as well as scrubs, washes, massages, and other treatments.

DAY 3 / MORNING

BREAKFAST   Breakfast is delicious at the **Mayflower Inn,** although it is not included in the room rate. Menu items include farm-fresh eggs prepared in a variety of ways, French toast, waffles, pastries, and lots of fresh fruit.

From Washington take Route 47 north to Route 202, turn left, and then turn right onto Route 45. About 2 miles up on the left, you'll come to North Shore Road. Turn onto it and take the second right onto Hopkins Road, which is home to **Hopkins Vineyard,** 25 Hopkins Rd., New Preston (860-868-7954; www.hopkinsvineyard .com). There are tours of the winery as well as tastings.

LUNCH   **The Boulders Inn,** East Shore Road, New Preston (860-868-0541; www.bouldersinn.com), starts serving "dinner" at noon on Sun. The fare is contemporary New England cuisine.

After lunch (or an early dinner) take a leisurely drive around the lake before heading back to New York City.

There's More . . . .

Bird-watching. There are plenty of opportunities to pull out the binoculars in the Litchfield area. Here are some of the best spots:

Audubon Center at Sharon, 325 Route 4, Sharon; (860) 364-0520; www.audubon.org.

Flanders Nature Center, office at Flanders Road, off Route 6, Woodbury; (860) 263-3711; www.flandersnaturecenter.org.

H. C. Barnes Memorial Nature Center, 175 Shrub Rd., Bristol; (860) 589-6082; www.elcct.org.

White Memorial Foundation, Route 202, Litchfield; (860) 567-0857; www.whitememorialcc.org.

Horseback riding. **Lee's Riding Stable, Inc.,** East Litchfield Road (off Route 118), Litchfield; (860) 567-0785.

Skiing. **Mohawk Mountain Ski Area,** Great Hollow Road, Cornwall; (860) 672-6100; www.mohawkmountain.com. Connecticut's largest ski resort, with twenty-three trails.

Special Events . . . .

JUNE
Laurel Festival, Winsted. Driving routes for viewing mountain laurels in bloom; laurel queen; parade. For more information, call (860) 379-2713.

MID-JUNE THROUGH MID-AUGUST.
Norfolk Chamber Music Festival, Norfolk. This annual festival takes place on the grounds of a charming 19th-century estate. For program and ticket information, call (203) 432-1966 between Sept

and May or (860) 542-3000 during June, July, and Aug or visit
www.yale.edu/norfolk.

JULY
Annual Litchfield Open House Tour, Litchfield. Tour includes Litchfield homes of historic and architectural interest. Call (860) 567-
9423 or visit www.litchfieldct.com.

SEPTEMBER
Connecticut Antique Machinery Fall Festival, Kent. An annual festival on the grounds of the Connecticut Antique Machinery Museum;
www.ctamachinery.com.

Other Recommended Restaurants and Lodgings . . . .

MORRIS
Winvian, 155 Alan White Rd.; (860) 567-9600; www.winvian.com.
From the road, this small and very high-end resort looks like a New
England farm 200 years ago. A collection of red and white buildings stands along with a saltbox house on 113 meadowed acres.
Enter the grounds, however, and you find yourself in a world that's
every inch new millennium, full of fantasy and sophistication. Fifteen New England architects contributed to the distinctly different
eighteen freestanding "cottages." Among the cottages is the Tree-
house, designed by John Connell, which is right out of a ten-year-
old boy's dreams; it is suspended between trees and stands 35 feet
off the ground. All the cottages have at least one wood-burning
fireplace, a screened porch, and large whirlpool tubs with separate
steam showers in the bathrooms.

NEW PRESTON

Boulders Inn, East Shore Road; (860) 868-0541; www.boulders inn.com. This country inn on Lake Waramaug has a selection of accommodations in the main house (built in 1895), the carriage house, and guesthouses.

The Hopkins Inn, Hopkins Road; (860) 868-7295; www.thehop kinsinn.com. Situated on the northern shore of Lake Waramaug, this is a pleasant inn with eleven guest rooms and two apartments for lodging.

For More Information . . . .

Connecticut Tourism Division, 505 Hudson St., Hartford, CT 06106; (860) 270-8080 or (800) 282-6863; www.ctbound.org.

Northwest Connecticut Convention and Visitors Bureau, P.O. Box 968, Litchfield, CT 06759; (860) 567-4506; www.northwestct .com.

NEW ENGLAND ESCAPE *Seven*

Newport
MASTS AND MANSIONS / 2 NIGHTS

Gleaming yachts, palatial mansions, tennis tournaments, Newport Jazz Festival—these are the things that come to most people's minds at the mere mention of Newport. This sensationally situated Rhode Island city (poised on the southern tip of Aquidneck Island and bounded by water on three sides) does offer a slice of the good life.

Oldest standing synagogue in the United States
Renowned restaurants
Opulent summer cottages
Historic waterfront
Tennis

Newport had two periods of history during which it enjoyed prominence. During colonial days it was a very important trade center. Later on, in the 19th-century Gilded Age, it became a popular resort for old-money families (including the Vanderbilts, Astors, and Belmonts) who built opulent summer "cottages" here.

Thanks to the Preservation Society of Newport County and the Newport Restoration Foundation, the history of Newport has been beautifully restored and preserved. During a short visit you can combine a walking tour of its colonial section in the northwest with a tour of its enormous mansions in the southern end.

Newport is a place you can go back to year after year, discovering new places or revisiting old ones. Squeezing everything into one weekend is a tall order, especially if you want to spend some time relaxing on a veranda or a breezy beach. Nevertheless, it's a reasonable amount of time to get an introduction.

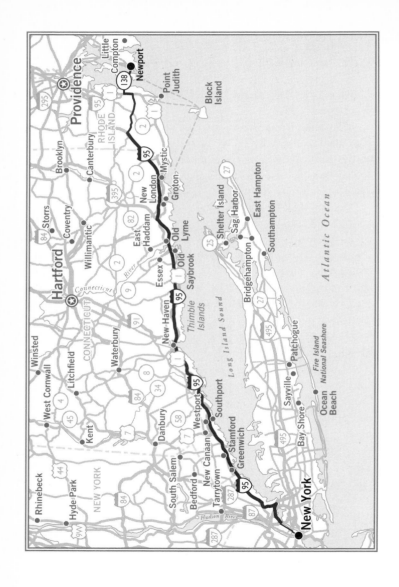

DAY 1 / MORNING

The fastest way to reach Newport from New York is to take I-95 North to exit 3A, Route 138 East, in Rhode Island. Follow Route 138 East over the Jamestown and Newport Bridges and directly into Newport.

First thing's first: Ditch your car. You'll spend the first day touring **Colonial Newport,** which can best be explored on foot. It's the northwestern section of the city, clustered around the harbor. You can't possibly do everything we've proposed, so be prepared to pick and choose as you go along.

A good starting point is Washington Street, which runs from Long Wharf to Battery Park and is lined with old gas lamps and colonial houses. From Washington Square walk north and make your first stop **Hunter House,** 54 Washington St. (401-847-1000; www.newportmansions.org). This colonial home dates from 1748 and has been faithfully restored inside and out. It's open from May through mid-Sept from 10 a.m. to 5 p.m. daily; tours are offered every hour on the hour.

From Hunter House walk north up Washington to Popular Street, where you'll turn right and follow to Farewell Street. Here there are several ancient cemeteries, including an 18th-century **Common Burial Ground** on Warner Street (a continuation of Popular Street on the other side of Farewell Street). From there walk south on Farewell Street to Thames Street until you reach Washington Square.

Here you'll find the **Museum of Newport History** at the Brick Market (Washington and Touro Streets; 401-841-0813; www.new porthistorical.org), which was built in 1760 and has been used in a variety of ways. For some time it was used as a theater, later on it was a town hall, and now it's an exhibit hall devoted to Newport history. It's open Mon and Wed through Sat from 10 a.m. to 5 p.m. and

Sun from 1 to 5 p.m. from Apr through Oct. Hours are 10 a.m. to 4 p.m. Fri and Sat and 1 to 4 p.m. Sun from Nov through Mar. Nearby you'll see the **Newport Colony House** on Washington Square (401-846-0813; www.newporthistorical.org), which was the headquarters of the colonial and state governments. The Declaration of Independence was read from the balcony of this building. In summer months there are tours starting at 10 a.m. every half hour Thurs, Fri, and Sat (last tour is 3:30 p.m.). Closed Sept to mid-June.

Newport's oldest house, the **Wanton–Lyman Hazard House,** is a couple of blocks away at 17 Broadway (401-846-0813). Here you'll find a museum, 18th-century cooking demonstrations, and a colonial garden. Hours are Thurs through Sat from 10 a.m. to 4 p.m. in summer (tours on the hour); other times by appointment.

The White Horse Tavern can be your next stop. Walk west on Broadway and north on Farewell to Marlborough Street; it's on the corner. This Newport landmark has been in operation since 1687.

LUNCH   **The White Horse Tavern,** 26 Marlborough St. (401-849-3600; www.whitehorsetavern.com), combines both historical charm (fireplaces, dark-beamed ceilings, slanting wood floors) and decent food (salads, seafood, some pasta dishes).

AFTERNOON

Nearby you'll find the **Great Friends Meeting House,** 29 Farewell St. (401-846-0813; www.newporthistorical.org), which dates from 1699. It's the oldest Quaker meetinghouse in America. It's open Thurs through Sat in summer, other times by appointment. Hourly tours start at 10 a.m.

From there walk back through Washington Square and turn left onto Touro Street, where you'll find the **Touro Synagogue,** 85 Touro

St. (401-847-4794; www.tourosynagogue.org), the oldest standing temple in the United States. Founded in 1658, it is a magnificent building with a rich history. Perhaps most notable is that in 1781, George Washington attended a town meeting here. Later he wrote a letter to the congregation that was an expression of religious liberty in America. In it, he said, "For happily the Government of the United States which gives to bigotry no sanction, to persecution no assistance, requires only that they who live under its protection should demean themselves as good citizens in giving it on all occasions their effectual support." Tours of the synagogue are offered every day except Sat. Open Thurs through Sat during the summer, 10 a.m. to 4 p.m. The **Newport Historical Society** (401-846-0813; www.newporthistorical.org) is a couple of doors down at 82 Touro St.. Many of the guided walking tours begin here. Inside there's a museum devoted to local history. Hours are Tues through Fri from 9:30 a.m. to 4:30 p.m. and Sat from 9:30 a.m. to noon.

Walk south down Division Street to the corner of Spring and Church Streets and you'll spot **Trinity Church** on Queen Anne Square (401-846-0660; www.trinitynewport.org), a beautiful example of colonial architecture. When it was built in 1726, it was hailed as "the most beautiful timber structure in America." It's open daily from 10 a.m. to 4 p.m.

Carry on east along Church Street to the **Redwood Library and Athenaeum,** 50 Bellevue Ave. (401-847-0292; www.redwood library.org) at the beginning of Bellevue Avenue. Not only is this the country's oldest library (founded in 1747) in continuous use, but it has a wonderful collection of Early American paintings inside. Guided tours are available Mon through Fri at 10:30 a.m. The library is otherwise open Tues through Thurs from 9:30 a.m. to 8 p.m., Mon, Fri, and Sat from 9:30 a.m. to 5:30 p.m., and Sun from 1 to 5 p.m.

The **Newport Art Museum and Art Association,** 76 Bellevue Ave. (401-848-8200; www.newportartmuseum.com), is on the next block. It showcases changing exhibits by contemporary New England artists. Memorial Day through Columbus Day, it's open Mon through Sat, 10 a.m. to 5 p.m., Sun noon to 5 p.m.; Columbus Day through Memorial Day, Mon through Sat, 10 a.m. to 4 p.m., Sun noon to 4 p.m.

DINNER   **Twenty-Two Bowens Wine Bar and Grille,** 22 Bowens Wharf (401-841-8884; www.22bowens.com) is a great choice for steak or seafood on the waterfront. It has thirty-five wines by the glass and more than 600 wine labels.

LODGING   For the ultimate short-but-sweet second honeymoon, consider the **Chanler at Cliff Walk,** 117 Memorial Blvd. (401-847-1300; www.thechanler.com). This magnificent oceanfront mansion was originally built in 1865 as the summer home for New York congressman John Winthrop Chanler and his wife, the former Margaret Astor Ward. Today it offers a collection of guest rooms that are every inch grand, each one with its own distinctive decor. Several reflect particular periods of history; among them are the Louis XVI Room, the Renaissance Room, and the Empire Room. There are also ocean villas with New England Island themes, including Martha's Vineyard, Nantucket, and Block Island. If you're traveling with children, consider staying at the **Hotel Viking** (One Bellevue Ave.; 401-847-3300; www.hotelviking.com), a historic redbrick hotel within easy walking distance of the many eateries on Thames Street. It has a pool for enjoying downtime.

DAY 2 / MORNING

BREAKFAST   If you're staying at the **Chanler,** continental breakfast—served in your room or downstairs in the restaurant—is part of the rate. At the **Hotel Viking,** you can get a traditional New England breakfast in One Bellevue, their restaurant.

Devote the bulk of the day to visiting some of the great Newport mansions. The "cottages" were built by such robber barons as the Vanderbilts and Belmonts in the late 19th century. Several of them have guided tours that last about an hour. Most of the mansions are open daily between 10 a.m. and 5 p.m. in summer; winter hours vary. There are a variety of ticket options which can be purchased online in advance. For example, the Newport Mansions Experience includes admission to five houses ($31 adults; $10 kids ages 6 to 17). The Breakers Plus ticket package includes admission to The Breakers and one other mansion ($23 adults; $6 for kids ages 6 to 17). Additionally, there are special tours offered over the holidays. For specific hours or to order tickets, visit www.newportmansions .com or call the Preservation Society of Newport County at (401) 847-1000.

You can start by visiting **Kingscote,** Bowery Street off Bellevue Avenue, which is relatively modest compared with some of the others. It was built in 1840 for a plantation owner. The **Elms,** which is a little farther south on Bellevue, is a classical building surrounded by formal gardens, fountains, and a sweeping lawn. It was built for a coal baron at the turn of the 20th century. Continue south on Bellevue and you'll come to **Château-sur-Mer,** which was the residence of William Shepard Wetmore, who made his fortune in the China trade. The most famous of the Newport mansions, the **Breakers,** is on Ochre Point Avenue (turn left on Victoria and continue to Ochre Point Avenue). This stunning property has seventy rooms. It was built in 1893 for Cornelius Vanderbilt II and his family. Return to Bellevue and continue south to **Rosecliff,** which has been used as a set for several movies, including *The Great Gatsby.* Farther south on Bellevue is the Astor's **Beechwood.** Here you can watch costumed actors and actresses re-create the lives of the Astor family, their guests, and staff. **Marble House** is the next stop continuing down Bellevue. This house, which must be seen to be believed, was designed by Beaux Arts-trained Richard Morris Hunt, whom William K. Vanderbilt asked to create "the very best living accommodations that money could buy." The last mansion to visit on Bellevue Avenue is **Belcourt Castle,** which is filled with European and oriental treasures.

LUNCH During the summer months the **Castle Hill Inn & Resort,** at 590 Ocean Dr. (401-849-3800; www.castlehillinn.com), serves a great Sunday brunch (reservations are a must). Other times of the year, your best bet is to head back into town and take your pick of great lunch spots.

AFTERNOON

Ocean Drive follows the coast past **Hammersmith Farm.** The childhood home of the late Jacqueline Bouvier Kennedy Onassis is now privately owned and no longer open to the public but sits up on a hill and can be seen from the road.

Nearby is the **Museum of Yachting,** Fort Adams State Park, Ocean Drive (401-847-1018; www.museumofyachting.org), which showcases highlights of the America's Cup and other sailing events. If you're traveling with children, check out the **Museum's Discovery Center,** where kids of all ages can experiment with hands-on stations and learn about boats, safety, construction, and sailing. There's also a sail-racing simulator and a wind tunnel that shows how a sail works. The museum is open daily from 10 a.m. to 5 p.m.

DINNER Newport has no shortage of great restaurants. An excellent downtown choice is **Restaurant Bouchard,** 505 Thames St. (401-846-0123; www .restaurantbouchard.com), which prides itself on its "creative classic" cuisine.

LODGING Return to your hotel.

DAY 3 / MORNING

BRUNCH   **The Clarke Cooke House** on Bannister's Wharf (401-849-2900; www.clarkecooke.com) serves a great selection of dishes for brunch on Sundays.

Plan to spend some time walking along the 3½ mile **Cliff Walk** (www.cliffwalk.com). Hugging the coastline, it dips and twists its way over cliffs, taking you past some of the town's most beautiful mansions. A National Recreation Trail, it's also a popular running or power-walking route. To reach it, park along Narragansett Avenue. It's open from dawn to dusk.

LUNCH   The Kobe burger at the **Spiced Pear Restaurant** at the Chanler Inn, 117 Memorial Blvd. (401-847-2244; www.spicedpear.com), was number three on GQ's "Twenty Burgers You Have to Try Before You Die" a while back. Made with chopped Kobe beef and topped with barbecued Kobe brisket and a tomato-onion jam, it lives up to that lofty accolade. After a stroll along the Cliff Walk, one end of which is right at the Chanler Inn, it's a great spot to pause for lunch and take in the view.

Then make your way over to the **International Tennis Hall of Fame** and the **Tennis Museum,** located in the Newport Casino, which was designed by McKim, Mead and White (194 Bellevue Ave.; 401-849-3990; www.tennisfame.com). The first National Tennis Championships were held here in 1881. The hall of fame and museum are open from 9:30 a.m. to 5 p.m. daily except Thanksgiving and Christmas. By the way, you don't have to be a member to play tennis here. Call for reservations (or just walk in—midday is best) and wear predominantly white tennis attire. Open for play through Sept; (401) 846-0642.

Afterwards, return to the wharves for a look around the shops before heading back to New York City (take Route 138 west back to I-95 and follow that south to the metropolitan area).

There's More . . . .

Beaches. **Newport Beach,** on Memorial Boulevard, and **King Park and Beach,** on Wellington Avenue, are open to the public. There's also a small beach at **Fort Adams State Park.**

Bikes. Bikes can be rented at **Ten-Speed Spokes,** 18 Elm St.; (401) 847-5609; www.tenspeedspokes.com.

Harbor Cruises. There are several boat cruises offered in Newport. You can take a sailboat cruise on the 78-foot schooner *Adirondack II* (contact the **Newport Yachting Center;** 401-846-3018; www.newport yachtingcenter.org). There are one-hour narrated tours of Newport Harbor and Narragansett Bay offered by **Oldport Marine** (401-847-9109; www.oldportmarine.com). **Classic Cruises of Newport** has harbor cruises on both the schooner Madeleine and the classic motor yacht Rum Runner II departing from Bannister's Wharf in the heart of downtown (401-849-3033; www.cruisenewport.com).

State Park. **Fort Adams State Park** on Ocean Drive surrounds Fort Adams. Here you can enjoy beach swimming, fishing, boating, and picnicking.

Topiary Garden. Giant green lions, bears, horses, and other animals are sculpted out of privet and yew at the **Green Animals Topiary Garden** (www.newportmansions.org). It's located on Cory's Lane in Portsmouth, off Route 114. Be sure to swing by this historic country estate on your way into or out of Newport.

Vintage Dinner Train. The **Newport Dinner Train** leaves the depot at 19 America's Cup Ave.; (401) 841-8700 or (800) 398-7427; www .newportdinnertrain.com. This is a vintage train designed to take passengers back to an era of grace and romance. As you cruise along enjoying the scenery out a picture window, you'll feast on a gourmet meal replete with crystal, china, and linen.

Walking Tours. **Newport on Foot Guided Tours** (401-846-5391) offers guided walking tours where you can step back in time and see landmarks, graveyards, colonial life, and architecture at an easy pace. **Newport 101 Walking Tours** (401-846-4464; www.newport 101.com) offers walking tours of a historic section of town. Both walking tour companies start their tours at the Visitor Center.

Special Events . . . .

MARCH
Newport Irish Heritage Month. Throughout the town there are a variety of events including concerts, plays, arts and crafts, a parade, and more.

MID-AUGUST
JVC Jazz Festival, Newport. Outdoor concerts by some of the world's best jazz musicians.

DECEMBER
Christmas in Newport. Month-long citywide celebration. Concerts, candlelight tours, Festival of Trees, Holly Ball, and visits by St. Nicholas. The Breakers, the Elms, and Marble House are decorated for the holidays.

New England Escape Seven

Other Recommended Restaurants and Lodgings . . . .

LITTLE COMPTON

Stone House, 122 Sakonnet Point Rd., Little Compton (401-635-2222; www.stonehouse1854.com). In nearby Little Compton, this historic property was originally a private estate built in 1854. Today, it's a very stylish hotel with a spa, a gourmet restaurant, and a revived Tap Room which was said to have been a speakeasy during Prohibition.

MIDDLETOWN

Flo's Clam Shack, 4 Wave Ave., Middletown; (401) 847-8141; www.flosclamshack.net. The place to go if you're in the mood for fried clams and oysters, lobster rolls, or raw shellfish.

NEWPORT

Francis Malbone House, 392 Thames St.; (401) 846-0392 or (800) 846-0392; www.malbone.com. A historic inn with eighteen antiques-filled rooms situated around a central garden. The building itself was designed in 1760.

Ivy Lodge, 12 Clay St.; (401) 849-6865 or (800) 834-8865; www.ivylodge.com. Right in the mansion district, this is a stately Victorian bed-and-breakfast with an impressive foyer by Stanford White. The Ivy Lodge welcomes children. It's just a block and a half from the Cliff Walk.

La Farge Perry House, 24 Kay St.; (401) 847-2223; www.lafargeperry.com. This is a very tasteful bed-and-breakfast not far from many of Newport's attractions. A three-story historic house, it is named for the painter and stained-glass artist John La Farge and his wife, Margaret Perry, who bought the house in 1861. There are five suites, including a family suite.

For More Information . . . .

Newport County Convention and Visitor's Bureau, 23 America's Cup Ave., Newport, RI 02840; (800) 976-5122; www.gonewport.com.

The Preservation Society of Newport County, 424 Bellevue Ave., Newport, RI 02840; (401) 847-1000; www.newportmansions.org.

Rhode Island Tourism Division Information Center, located on I-95 north in Richmond, just north of the Rhode Island/Connecticut state line. Open seven days a week, year-round; (800) 556-2484; www.visitrhodeisland.com.

NEW ENGLAND ESCAPE *Eight*
Block Island—With or Without a Car
OFFSHORE TOURING / 2 NIGHTS

Beaches
Bicycling
Seafood
Art galleries
Lighthouses

Anchored 12 miles off the coast of mainland Rhode Island, this bite-size island (a mere 11 square miles) is strewn with wildflowers, dotted with shingled cottages and placid pools, crisscrossed by hundreds of miles of stone walls, surrounded by white, duney beaches, and, on one coast, edged by cliffs that rise 200 feet above the sea. The Old Harbor Village (its ferry port) is filled with Victorian buildings and is a National Register Historic Site.

During summer months the island is its liveliest, with at least half a dozen ferries a day shuttling day-trippers over from the mainland. Most of them don't get much farther than Water Street and the nearby beaches, however, which leaves the rest of the island blissfully peaceful. Unlike some northeastern islands, Block Island has not fallen prey to the customary tourist trappings such as fast-food chains and tacky souvenir shops. In fact, there are not even any traffic lights on the island.

If you want to experience the island as the locals do, consider visiting during a weekend in Oct, when there's a slight nip in the air and not another tourist in sight.

Whatever time of year you go, for a short visit, your best bet is to leave your car on the mainland, ferry over, and rent bikes to get around. You can take a ferry from the Galilee State Pier in **Point Judith,** year-round, or from New London (Connecticut), Providence, or Newport during the summer months. There are also ferries from Montauk, Long Island, New York.

NEW ENGLAND ESCAPE *Nine*

The Berkshires
MUSIC, MANSIONS, AND MORE / 2 NIGHTS

The Berkshire Hills are known for both their rural beauty (sprawling farms, tidy little villages, dozen of lakes and ponds, thousands of acres of forest) and their cultural assets (they're home to the Tanglewood Music Festival and Jacob's Pillow Dance Festival). Located in the western quarter of Massachusetts, they stretch all the way from Connecticut to Vermont (just

> Rural scenery
> Performing arts
> Hiking
> Historical homes
> Antiques and crafts shops
> Galleries
> Fine dining
> Country inns

south of the Green Mountains). The area, which is now massively popular for weekenders, especially during the summer months, first became famous when Nathaniel Hawthorne wrote *Tanglewood Tales.* Route 7 takes you right through the heart of them, passing through a series of wonderful little towns, including Stockbridge, Lenox, Pittsfield, and Williamstown.

During July and August, when the Tanglewood Music Festival and the area's other performing arts are in full bloom, the Berkshires can be very crowded. Many inns require a three-night minimum stay, and there are long waits at restaurants and cultural attractions. Your best bet is to visit midweek.

DAY 1 / MORNING

Head north on I-684, then east on I-84 to Route 7 north. Route 7 takes you right to the southern Berkshires.

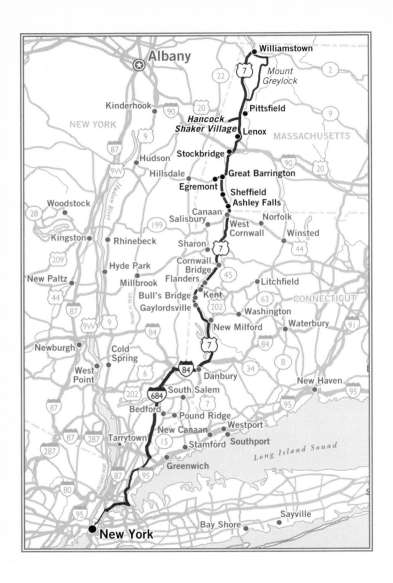

Shortly after you cross over the Connecticut border into Massachusetts, turn onto Route 7A to reach **Ashley Falls.** Follow the signs from the center of Ashley Falls to your first stop, **Bartholomew's Cobble** (413-229-8600), a 294-acre preserve of 500-million-year-old marble outcroppings above the Housatonic River. You can stretch your legs a bit by following the Ledges Interpretive Trail, which introduces you to some of the preserve's amazing variety of plants and flowers. Trails are open daily, year-round, from sunrise to sunset. Just across a field (you'll see signs) is the **Colonel John Ashley House** (also 413-229-8600), which dates from 1735, making it one of the oldest houses in the county. It's open from Memorial Day weekend through Columbus Day, Sat and Sun only, plus those two Mondays, from 1 to 5 p.m. You can find more information on both Bartholomew's Cobble and the Colonel John Ashley House by visiting www.thetrustees.org.

Continue north on Route 7A to get back on Route 7 and to **Sheffield,** your next stop. This town is crammed with antiques shops (a directory of who sells what is available in each one). Sheffield is also home to the state's oldest covered bridge (look for the red sign on the right).

Once you've done the shops of Sheffield, carry on to Great Barrington, where you can poke around some shops and stop for lunch.

LUNCH   **Rubi's Coffee and Sandwiches,** 264 Main St.; (413) 528-0488 is right behind (and related to) Rubiner's Cheesemonger and Grocers. You can have a great simple lunch here.

AFTERNOON

After lunch continue north on Route 7 for about another 4 miles until you see **Monument Mountain** looming before you. If you're feeling up for it, take time out to hike to the summit. Be prepared, however; it could take about two or three hours.

The next stop is **Stockbridge,** which many people know from Norman Rockwell's famous illustrations that first appeared on the covers of the *Saturday Evening Post* and *McCall's.* You can see some of the original covers as well as the world's largest collection of the illustrator's works in the **Norman Rockwell Museum,** Route 183 (413-298-4100; www.nrm.org). Hours are 10 a.m. to 5 p.m. daily from May through Oct and 10 a.m. to 4 p.m. Mon through Fri and 10 a.m. to 5 p.m. Sat and Sun from Nov through Apr. Just up the road from the museum is **Chesterwood,** Route 183 (413-298-3579; www.chesterwood.org), the summer home of Daniel Chester French, who sculpted the seated Lincoln in the Lincoln Memorial. The museum is open daily from 10 a.m. to 5 p.m. from May through Oct. There are house and studio tours as well as gardens and a museum of the artist's works. Two other top Stockbridge attractions are the **Mission House,** Main Street (413-298-3239), which houses a fine collection of Early American furnishings, and **Naumkeag,** Prospect Hill Road (414-298-3239), a summer "cottage" that was used during the 19th-century "gilded era" when families such as the Vanderbilts and Westinghouses vacationed in these hills. Both the Mission House and Naumkeag are open daily from 10 a.m. to 5 p.m. from Memorial Day to Columbus Day; last tour at 4 p.m. For additional information on Mission House and Naumkeag, visit www.thetrustees.org.

The **Red Lion Inn,** 30 Main St. (413-298-5545; www .redlioninn.com), has been a major Stockbridge landmark for more than 200 years. Consider stopping in for a drink in the courtyard or on one of the rockers on the front porch. Then wander around the shops that crowd around Main Street.

DINNER Choose the **Old Mill,** Route 23, South Egremont (413-528-1421), which was once a blacksmith's shop as well as a mill. It's one of the most highly regarded restaurants in the Berkshires, with a good selection of fish, chicken, and steak dishes. An alternative is the **Castle Street Cafe,** 10 Castle St., Great Barrington (413-528-5244; www.castlestreetcafe.com), a popular bistro (reservations are a must) known for its deliriously good pasta and grilled fish dishes.

LODGING Year-round it's important to make reservations at Berkshire inns. During the busy months expect to find many places full. **The Red Lion Inn,** which was originally built in 1773 as a stagecoach stop, is a New England classic.

EVENING

In addition to Tanglewood (just north of Stockbridge in Lenox; www.bso.org) and Jacob's Pillow (east of Stockbridge in Becket; www.jacobspillow.org), the southern Berkshires have an abundance of other shows and cultural events. For program information and tickets, call ahead: Berkshire Choral Institute (413-229-8526; www.chorus.org); Aston Magna Festival (413-528-3595; www.astonmagna.org); Berkshire Opera Company (413-644-9000; www.berkop.org); Stockbridge Summer Music Series (413-443-1138; www.baygo.com/ssms); and DeSisto Estate Dinner Theatre and Cabaret (413-298-4032).

DAY 2 / MORNING

BREAKFAST Enjoy a continental breakfast of oatmeal, granola, bagels, and fruit at the **Red Lion Inn.**

Afterward head north out of Stockbridge on Route 7. About 5 miles up, at the junction of Routes 7 and 7A, you'll find **The Mount,** 2 Plunkett St. at the south junction of Routes 7 and 7A, Lenox (413-637-1899; www.edithwharton.org), which was the summer residence of novelist Edith Wharton. The house, a classical revival, is sensationally situated on 49 acres. It's open daily between early June and early Nov, 9 a.m. to 5 p.m. (house) or 9 a.m. to 6 p.m. (grounds).

Follow Route 7A to **Lenox,** which is home to **Tanglewood,** on West Street (413-637-1600; www.bso.org), where legendary music can be heard under the stars throughout the summer months. Tanglewood is the summer home for the **Boston Symphony Orchestra.** If you're not planning to attend a performance, do take time to stroll around the grounds (there are 210 acres including formal gardens), which are open daily.

LUNCH **Church Street Cafe,** 65 Church St. (413-637-2745; www .churchstreetcafe.biz), is a very successful bistro with all sorts of eclectic and eth-nic dishes. Try to get a table outside if the weather's nice (closed Sun and Mon from Oct through May).

AFTERNOON

From Lenox drive north on Route 7, making a stop at the **Berkshire Museum** in **Pittsfield,** right on Route 7 (locally known as South Street) at 39 South St. (413-443-7171; www.berkshiremuseum .org). It has a good collection of 19th- and 20th-century paintings as well as some local exhibits. It's open Mon through Sat from 10 a.m. to 5 p.m. and Sun from noon to 5 p.m. Also in Pittsfield is **Arrowhead,** 780 Holmes Rd. (413-442-1793; www.mobydick .org), the house where Herman Melville wrote Moby Dick, along with three other novels. It's open from Memorial Day through Oct 31 daily from 9:30 a.m. to 5 p.m., and by appointment only the rest of the year.

About 5 miles west of Pittsfield (at the junction of Routes 20 and 41) is **Hancock Shaker Village** (413-443-0188; www.hancock shakervillage.org), a living-history museum devoted to the Shakers. For about 180 years (1781–1960), the site was a Shaker community. It's open daily year-round. Late Oct through the Sun of Memorial Day weekend, hours are 10 a.m. to 3 p.m. From Memorial Day to late Oct, hours are 9:30 a.m. to 5 p.m.

Carry on to **Williamstown,** which is not far from the Vermont border. Among the town's most notable attractions are the **Sterling and Francine Clark Art Institute,** 225 South St. (413-597-3131; www.williams.edu), home to the Williams College Museum of Art (WCMA), which has 12,000 works that span the history of art, as well as one of the nation's best collections of rare books.

Press on another 5 miles east (following Route 2) to the former factory town of North Adams, where you'll find a great place to stay as well as the Massachusetts Museum of Contemporary Art and a pleasing selection of restaurants.

DINNER   **Gramercy Bistro,** 24 Marshall St. (413-663-5300; www .gramercybistro.com) prides itself on using local produce in its many very creative dishes.

LODGING   **The Porches Inn** at MASS MoCA, 231 River St. (413-664-0400; www.porches.com) is right across the street from the Massachusetts Museum of Contemporary Art and is a work of art itself—original and uniquely stylish. Its forty-seven rooms and suites, along with stunning public spaces, are a clever marriage of retro and contemporary design.

EVENING

During summer months the **Williamstown Theatre Festival** brings professionals and apprentices together for traditional and experimental theater. For program and ticket information, call (413) 597-3400; www.wtfestival.org.

DAY 3 / MORNING

BREAKFAST   A European continental buffet is part of the room rate at the **Porches** and is a perfect prelude to touring the Mass MoCA.

The largest mill complex of North Adams has been converted to the **Massachusetts Museum of Contemporary Art** (1040 Mass MoCA Way, 413-662-2111; www.massmoca.org), which is a phenomenally hip museum. Check ahead for the schedule of films and events. Otherwise, stuff yourself on cutting-edge sculpture and installation art.

Heading west on Route 2, just outside of North Adams, you'll see a sign at Notch Road that indicates the northern entrance to the **Mount Greylock** reservation (413-499-4262; www.mass.gov). The ride to the top of the state's highest peak (3,491 feet) takes about half an hour and offers a five-state view. At the summit there's a rustic stone-and-wood lodge called **Bascom Lodge** (413-743-1591; www.naturesclassroom.org) that's run by the Appalachian Mountain Club. The lodge can accommodate thirty-two guests overnight. Follow the road back down and you'll wind up in Lanesborough on Route 7, just north of Pittsfield.

Continue south on Route 7, stopping at farm stands along the way to stock up on fresh produce and dairy. Chances are that you'll also see signs for tag sales, at which you may or may not unearth some worthwhile finds. Trace your steps back to Manhattan, taking Route 7 to I-84 west to I-684 south.

There's More . . . .

Botanical gardens. The **Berkshire Botanical Garden,** Routes 102 and 183, Stockbridge; (413) 298-3926; www.berkshirebotanical .org. A refuge of beauty with a vast variety of plantings in a terraced herb garden, a pond garden, a rock garden, an ornamental vegetable garden, a children's garden (among others), and an arboretum and woodland interpretive trail. Open May through Oct daily from 10 a.m. to 5 p.m.

Historic railroad. **Berkshire Scenic Railway Museum,** Willow Creek Road, Lenox; (413) 637-2210; www.berkshirescenicrailroad.org. Railroad museum and vintage train rides. Museum open from 10 a.m. to 4 p.m. Memorial Day weekend through Oct.

Nature trails. Northwest of Lenox is the **Pleasant Valley Sanctuary** (www.massaudubon.org), which offers several miles of trails to explore. It's open Tues through Sun from dawn to dusk.

Skiing. There's downhill skiing at **Butternut Basin** (www.butternut basin.com), which is about 2 miles east of Great Barrington; **Jiminy Peak** in Hancock (www.jiminypeak.com); **Brodie Mountain** in New Ashford (www.brodiemountain.com); and other locations throughout the Berkshires.

Waterfalls. **Bash Bish Falls,** (413-528-0330; www.mass.gov), 12 miles southwest of South Egremont (just over the New York line), is a spectacularly scenic valley pierced by 50-foot Bash Bish Falls. A hiker's must at any time of year.

Special Events . . . .

LATE JANUARY
Lenox Winter Event. A 10K cross-country ski race in Kennedy Park in Lenox.

LATE JUNE THROUGH LATE AUGUST
Berkshire Theatre Festival, at the Berkshire Playhouse, East Main Street in Stockbridge. New and experimental theater. For program information and to order tickets, visit www.berkshiretheatre.org or call (866) 811-4111.

Williamstown Theatre Festival, Modern classics, contemporary plays, cabarets, and other performances. Call (413) 597-3400 or visit www.wtfestival.org for program and ticket information.

FOURTH OF JULY WEEKEND
The Berkshire Arts Festival, at Ski Butternut, Great Barrington. Every year An American Craftsman Galleries hosts this festival, which draws 10,000 to 12,000 visitors. For more information, call (413) 298-0175 or visit www.anamericancraftsman.com.

MID-JULY
Berkshire Charity Auto Show, Pittsfield. More than 500 antique and special-interest autos are displayed on the grounds of Hillcrest Hospital on West Street. Visit www.berkshireunitedway.com.

JULY THROUGH AUGUST
Aston Magna Festival, Great Barrington; (413) 528-3595; www.astonmagna.org. This summer festival takes place at St. James Church on Main Street.

The Berkshire Choral Festival (413-229-8526; www.chorus.org) offers five weeks of classical music at the Berkshire School concert shed.

Jacob's Pillow Dance Festival, Becket. A summer dance festival featuring ballet, modern dance, jazz, and mime. Contact Jacob's Pillow Dance Festival, (413) 243-0745; www.jacobspillow.org.

Tanglewood Music Festival, Lenox. Summer home of the Boston Symphony Orchestra. Outdoor concerts. Visit www.bso.org or call (617) 266-1492. During July and Aug only, you can call Tanglewood directly at (413) 637-1940.

MID-AUGUST
Sheffield Antiques Show, Sheffield. More than two dozen dealers from around the Northeast display their prize pieces at this annual event at the Mount Everett Regional High School on Berkshire School Road.

SEPTEMBER
Apple Squeeze Festival, Lenox. Celebration-of-apples festival.

Barrington Fair, Great Barrington. An annual fair with exhibits, agricultural displays, livestock, and entertainment.

EARLY OCTOBER
Autumn Weekend, Hancock Shaker Village, Pittsfield. Demonstrations of Shaker fall harvest activities. Visit www.hancockshakervillage.org.

LATE DECEMBER
House tours of Lenox. Usually the last Sat of Dec.

Other Recommended Restaurants and Lodgings . . . .

LENOX

Blantyre, 16 Blantyre Rd.; (413) 637-3556; www.blantyre.com. A 1905 replica of a Scottish castle, this is a magnificently scenic setting for both staying and dining.

Canyon Ranch in the Berkshires, 165 Kemble St.; (413) 637-4100 or (800) 742-9000; www.canyonranch.com. One of the best spas in the country. Consider spending a couple of nights here, dipping into its various spa treatments.

Cranwell Resort, Spa, and Golf Club, 55 Lee Rd.; (413) 637-1364; www.cranwell.com. The centerpiece of this resort is an elegant mansion that dates back to the Gilded Age of the late 19th century and is listed on the National Register of Historic Places. The resort is set on a 385-acre site designed by Frederick Law Olmsted.

Wheatleigh, West Hawthorne Road; (413) 637-0610 or (800) 321-0610; www.wheatleigh.com. This villa, built in 16th-century Florentine style, once belonged to a contessa. Today it's one of the Berkshires' most luxurious places to stay.

STOCKBRIDGE

The Inn at Stockbridge, Route 7; (888) 466-7865; www.stock bridgeinn.com. Within easy reach of all the area attractions, the Inn at Stockbridge offers a wonderful reprieve on twelve acres.

WILLIAMSTOWN

The Guest House at Field Farm, 554 Sloan Rd.; (413) 458-3135; http://guesthouseatfieldfarm.thetrustees.org. This is a stunning bed-and-breakfast filled with modern art and furnishings. The

1948 Bauhaus-inspired house was designed by Edwin Goodell Jr. for Lawrence and Eleanor Bloedel, modern-art collectors of the time. It's set on Field Farm, which sprawls over 316 acres.

For More Information . . . .

Berkshire Visitors Bureau, 3 Hoosac St., Adams, MA 01220; (413) 743-4500 or (800) 237-5747; www.berkshires.org.

Massachusetts Office of Travel and Tourism, 10 Park Plaza, Suite 4510, Boston, MA 02116; (617) 973-8500 or (800) 227-6277; www.mass-vacation.com.

NEW ENGLAND ESCAPE *Ten*

Southern Vermont

SMALL TOWNS AND MOUNTAIN SCENERY / 2 NIGHTS

Picturesque New England villages

Art galleries and museums

Designer outlets

Historic houses

Winter sports

Sophisticated restaurants

Nearly every inch of Vermont is New England just as you pictured it—covered bridges, immaculate dairy farms, steepled villages, and sagging old farmhouses where big-pawed yellow labs sleep on front porches. Add to that the fact that every season has its own appealing aspects, and choosing exactly when and where to go can be a happy dilemma.

Fortunately, you can't go wrong with Vermont. In the fall, the Crayola colors are everywhere (especially early to mid-October). At that time of year, the weather is often phenomenally beautiful, with flawless blue skies and plenty of sunshine. During winter the hills are alive with skiers and snowshoers. When the snows thaw, the landscape awakens into a profusion of blossoms and green. There's green everywhere, getting greener and greener each day as the state warms into summer.

In Vermont you're also never far from a high-quality cultural experience. For this escape we take you to the southern part of the state, overnighting in two of New England's most picturesque towns.

DAY 1 / MORNING

Try to get an early start so you can enjoy the myriad attractions in this part of the state. It'll take about four hours to reach

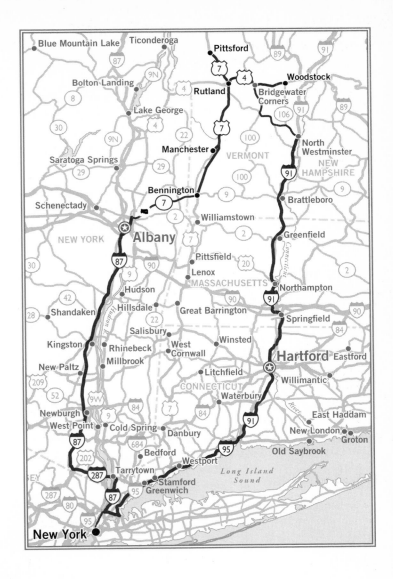

Manchester, your home for the night. From New York, take I-87 north to exit 23. Then get on I-787 north to Route 7 east. Follow Route 7 east to Route 279 east. Follow that to the end and look for signs to Vermont's Route 7 north, toward Manchester. Take Route 7 north to exit 3, then turn left onto Route 313. Make a right onto historic Route 7A north. Follow that for about 9 miles into Manchester.

Manchester was first "discovered" by visitors as a summer resort town in the 19th century. It was "rediscovered" in the 20th century as a hub for designer outlets. It's been called "the Fifth Avenue of the Mountains," so don't be discouraged when you see store after store in parts of town. Manchester also has a major historic claim to fame. Robert Todd Lincoln, eldest son of Abraham Lincoln, built a Georgian Revival mansion here in 1905 and called it **Hildene** (Route 7A; 802-362-1788; www.hildene.org). It's set on more than 400 acres, which you can tour on nature trails year-round (on skis come winter). The house is open for touring from mid-May through Oct.

LUNCH   **The Little Rooster Cafe,** Route 7A south in Manchester Center (802-362-3496) serves great sandwiches, crab cakes, and much more. Consider coming back for breakfast.

AFTERNOON

After lunch head over to the **Southern Vermont Arts Center** (West Road; 802-362-1405; www.svac.org), where you can stuff yourself on the great paintings of Reginald Marsh, Luigi Lucioni, Grandma Moses, and many others in its ten galleries.

Later, if you're up for a real adventure, you can acquire some skills of climbing rocks and crossing rolling logs in a Hummer H2 or Land Rover Discovery at the **Equinox Resort Off-Road Driving School** (www.equinoxresort.com). They have an 80-acre course and offer one- and two-hour lessons, for between one and four people.

DINNER   The Perfect Wife (2594 Depot St., Manchester Center; 802-362-2817; www.perfectwife.com) is a great choice for lunch. Referring to itself as "not just another pretty face," it serves lots of great seafood, meat dishes, and inventive salads. A great entree to try is the Howling Wolf Special, which includes steamed veggies, whole-grain pilaf, and roasted yams topped with yellow curry satay sauce and sun-dried cherry chutney.

LODGING   The Equinox, Historic Route 7A; 802-362-4700; www.equinoxresort.com. This is a very grand country hotel with a state-of-the-art spa, a wonderful selection of restaurants, and elegantly furnished guest rooms.

DAY 2 / MORNING

BREAKFAST   Your best bet is to stay put at the **Equinox** and treat yourself to a gourmet breakfast.

Afterward, follow Route 7 north to **Rutland,** which is home to several worthwhile attractions. Among them is the **Chaffee Center for Visual Arts** (16 South Main St.; 802-775-0356; www.chaffeeart center.org). Throughout the year there are changing exhibits of various artists' works in virtually all media (from watercolors and oils to printmaking and fine furniture). To see who is exhibiting while you're in town, visit the Center's Web site. There's also a **Norman Rockwell Museum** (654 Route 4 East; 877-773-6095; www.normanrockwellvt.com) here, with hundreds of magazine covers, advertisements, calendars, and other works by the beloved illustrator.

Just north of Rutland (take Route 7 to Pittsford) is the **New England Maple Museum** (Route 7, Pittsford; 802-483-9414; www.maplemuseum.com), where the history of maple sugaring is brought to life in exhibits, tours, and tastings.

The historic village of **Woodstock**—which Ladies Home Journal called "the prettiest small town in America"—is east of Rutland (follow Route 4). In town, take time to poke about the old-fashioned general store, antiques shops, and galleries.

LUNCH Right in the middle of town, you can't miss **Bentley's** (3 Elm St.; 802-457-3232; www.bentleysrestaurant.com), which has a lively atmosphere and serves burgers, salads, pasta dishes, and more.

AFTERNOON

Right outside of town you'll find **Billings Farm** (Route 12 and River Road; 802-457-2355; www.billingsfarm.org), a first-class farm-life museum. It's a dairy farm where you and your kids can help feed a Jersey cow, try churning some butter, and—come winter—enjoy a horse-drawn sleigh ride. (NOTE: The farm is open only limited dates throughout the winter, so check their Web site before going.) About 6 miles east of town is the **Sugarbush Farm** (591 Sugarbush Farm Rd., Woodstock; 802-457-1757; www.sugarbushfarm.com), where you can see how cheese is cut and waxed and learn all about maple sugaring.

Woodstock is also home to **Suicide Six,** which might just be the warmest and fuzziest alpine ski area you'll find in New England. There's a wonderful fireplace in the base lodge that's always crackling. Back in 1934, history was made here when a group of locals rigged a Model T Ford engine to power America's first ski tow.

DINNER There are several very good dining choices right at the **Woodstock Inn and Resort** (14 The Green; 802-457-1100; www.woodstockinn .com). If you're traveling with kids and want something super-casual, choose the Red Rooster Richardson's Tavern is a great spot for a burger (on weekends, sometimes local musicians perform). The Dining Room is an elegant alternative where you can settle down for a multi-course meal.

LODGING The **Woodstock Inn and Resort** is a big country inn in the center of town with a wonderful warm-and-fuzzy feel. This is apparent the moment you walk in and see the huge hearth, around which guests congregate on big, comfy couches. The resort has an extensive health and fitness center and a golf course that becomes a cross-country ski center in winter.

DAY 3 / MORNING

BREAKFAST You can serve yourself at the buffet or order off the menu at the Red Rooster right downstairs at the **Woodstock Inn.**

Afterward, pack up and meander south through the state, soaking up the scenery. From Woodstock, follow Route 4 west to Route 100A, which will take you right to **President Coolidge's Birthplace** (3780 Route 100A, Plymouth; 802-672-3773; www.historicvermont .org/coolidge). The boyhood home of the thirtieth president of the United States can be toured from late May to mid-Oct. Carry on south on Route 100 through Ludlow and then take Route 121 to Grafton, a quiet, tree-lined village with beautifully restored 19th-century buildings.

LUNCH **Daniels House Cafe** at the Daniels House, 92 Main St. (802-843-2255) is a perfect spot for a simple lunch—salads, soups, sandwiches, and the like.

AFTERNOON

From the cafe, it's a short drive east to I-91. Take I-91 south all the way to I-95, then follow I-95 back to New York.

There's More . . . .

City exploring. In Bennington there's an entire gallery devoted to the life and works of Grandma Moses at the **Bennington Museum** (www.benningtonmuseum.com/grandmagallery.html). There is also the first and only covered-bridge museum in the world at the **Bennington Center for the Arts** (www.benningtoncenterforthearts.org). Additionally, at Historic Potter's Yard you can take a tour and see **Bennington Potters** (www.benningtonpotters.com) at work. They are the largest working craft potters in the United States.

Skiing and other winter sports. The Green Mountain State is peppered with ski areas—both downhill and cross-country. In southern Vermont alone there are many, including **Mount Snow** (www .mountsnow.com), which is under an hour away once you cross the Vermont border. In addition to great skiing, it has tubing, snowmobile tours, snowshoeing, and spa services. **Stratton** (www.stratton.com) has major big-mountain skiing and snowboarding, with ninety trails, over a hundred acres of glades, and six terrain parks. **Bromley** (www.bromley.com) is a great family destination and has all sorts of money-saving packages. **Okemo** (www.okemo.com) has a grand total of 117 trails, along with lots of high-speed express lifts plus six terrain parks. **Killington** (www.killington.com) stretches across seven mountain areas (including Pico Mountain) and has access to 200 trails and 33 lifts with just one ticket. It's also home to the highest lift-served peak in Vermont—4,241-foot Killington Peak.

In Woodstock you'll find Suicide Six, which is a small ski area with a lot of charm plus the groomed trails of the **Woodstock Ski Touring Center** (www.woodstockinn.com). Among many southern Vermont cross-country centers is **Grafton Ponds Nordic Center** (www.graftonponds.com) in Grafton, with 30 kilometers of groomed trails along with 30 kilometers of back-country trails. Tucked away in the woods of Peru is the **Wild Wings Touring Center** (www.wildwingsski.com), with 25 kilometers groomed for classic. In Manchester, **Hildene Ski Touring Center** (www.hildene.org) has 15 kilometers of trails on the grounds of a historic house museum built by Robert Todd Lincoln as a summer home. The Carriage Barn is a warming hut for the ski center.

And that's not even all of them. To find the most comprehensive listing and details about downhill and cross-country centers in the state, go to www.skivermont.com.

Special Events . . . .

MAY

Plowing Match, Billings Farm and Museum, Woodstock; (802) 457-2355. Dozens of teamsters compete with their draft horses and oxen.

JUNE

Antique and Classic Car Show. Held on the grounds of Hildene (www.hildene.org), the show features antique and classic cars, vintage trucks, a flea market, toy car show, a parade, and food vendors. For more information, contact the Manchester Chamber of Commerce, 5046 Main St., Manchester Village, VT 05255; (802) 362-2100; www.manchestervermont.net.

AUGUST

Southern Vermont Art and Craft Festival, at Hildene (www.hildene .org). One-of-a-kind and limited-edition works, craft demonstrations, and food. Contact Craftproducers Markets, Inc. at (802) 425-3399 for more information; www.craftproducers.com.

NOVEMBER

Thanksgiving Weekend, Billings Farm and Museum, Woodstock; (802) 457-2355. Costumed guides prepare a 19th-century feast in the 1890 farmhouse. Activities—including horse-drawn wagon rides—for all ages.

For More Information . . . .

Manchester Regional Chamber of Commerce, 5046 Main St., Manchester Village, VT 05255; (802) 362-2100; www.manchesterver mont.net.

Ski Vermont, 26 State St., Montpelier, VT 05601; (802) 223-2439; www.skivermont.com.

Vermont Department of Tourism, 6 Baldwin St., Montpelier, VT 05602; (802) 828-3236; www.travel-vermont.com.

Woodstock Area Chamber of Commerce, P.O. Box 486, Woodstock, VT 05091; (888) 496-6378; www.woodstockvt.com.

MID-ATLANTIC *ESCAPES*

MID-ATLANTIC ESCAPE *One*

Spring Lake
A SMALL SHORE TOWN / 1 NIGHT

Nineteenth-century
  architecture
Beaches
Boardwalk
Seafood
Antiques shopping

About equidistant from Philadelphia and New York City, you'll find Spring Lake, one of the most pleasant towns on the Jersey Shore. Since the early part of last century, it has been a vacation spot for travelers wanting to get away from both cities. Back then they came by carriage and stayed in what was the grandest hotel (but no longer exists)—the Monmouth House. There are several buildings that do live on from that era, however, including an impressive collection of Victorian "cottages."

For this trip we suggest driving down in the morning (the drive takes not much more than an hour), spending the day and night enjoying the simple pleasures of Spring Lake, and then slowly meandering back to the city, stopping in Red Bank en route.

DAY 1 / MORNING

Take exit 98 off the Garden State Parkway to Route 34 south. Go 1½ miles to the traffic circle and turn left onto Route 524. Follow Route 524 for about 3 miles, and it'll take you right into town.

One of the best ways to enjoy **Spring Lake** is to just stroll leisurely. A good starting place is the boardwalk, which stretches 2 miles along the ocean and is not colonized by arcades and the other amusements found at so many other boardwalks.

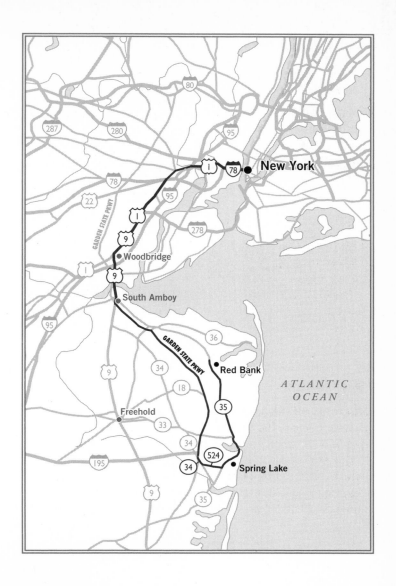

LUNCH   Right across from the boardwalk is the **Breakers,** Ocean and Newark Avenue (732-449-7700; www.breakershotel.com), where you can get a light lunch of sandwiches, salads, and burgers.

AFTERNOON

From the boardwalk you can wander through the wide, tree-lined streets of town, admiring one beautiful house after another. The lake for which the town is named is right in the center of town, surrounded by a park.

Spend whatever time is left swimming or sunning yourself on the beach, which is half a block from your hotel.

DINNER   **The Old Mill Inn,** Old Mill Road, Spring Lake Heights (732-449-1800 or 800-803-9031; www.oldmillinn.com), serves unfailingly good seafood and other American dishes. Many consider it a New Jersey institution.

LODGING   **Sea Crest by the Sea,** 19 Tuttle Ave. (732-449-9031 or 800-803-9031; www.seacrestbythesea.com), is an eleven-room Victorian guest house just half a block from the beach. All rooms are handsomely decorated with French and English furnishings from the 1880s.

DAY 2 / MORNING

If you're a jogger, consider lacing up your shoes and following the paths around the lake or running along the boardwalk, breathing in the invigorating ocean air.

BREAKFAST   Continental breakfast is included in the room price at **Sea Crest.**

After a leisurely breakfast and some more time spent relaxing on the beach or playing croquet at Sea Crest, head north back toward Manhattan, taking time out to explore **Red Bank.** Poised on the shores of the Navesink River, Red Bank is a historic community with lots of shops. If you're interested in antiques, it's home to a major **Antiques Center,** along West Front Street and Shrewsbury Avenue.

From there you can easily pick up the Garden State Parkway north to return to Manhattan.

There's More . . . .

Horse country. Slightly inland and just to the north of the Spring Lake area is a little chunk of horse country. The farms are in full view from the road and are concentrated in a little triangle of towns: Holmdel, Freehold, and Colt's Neck. Many of the farms can be seen along Routes 537, 79, 520, and 34.

Special Events . . . .

SUMMER MONTHS
Throughout the summer months, there are model-boat regattas on the lake on Sunday, croquet at Green Gables on Thursday, and weekly concerts in Potter Park. Check the Shore Holiday News for listings.

Other Recommended Restaurants and Lodgings . . . .

RUMSON
Fromagerie, 26 Ridge Rd.; (732) 842-8088; www.fromagerieres taurant.com. This is one of the Jersey Shore's most outstanding

restaurants. The food is French, the service very gracious, and the atmosphere elegant. Rumson is a short drive east of Red Bank.

SPRING LAKE

The Château Inn and Suites, 500 Warren Ave.; (732) 974-2000 or (877) 974-5253; www.chateauinn.com. A renovated Victorian hotel with forty rooms. The beach is 4 blocks away.

Normandy Inn, 21 Tuttle Ave.; (732) 449-7172; www.normandy inn.com. Listed on the National Register of Historic Places, this Italianate villa with Queen Anne modifications is an architectural gem. The furnishings date to the period of the house, which transports one back in time. There's an afternoon tea served along with home-baked goodies.

For More Information . . . .

Eastern Monmouth Area Chamber of Commerce, 170 Broad St., Red Bank, NJ 07701; (732) 741-0055; www.emacc.org.

New Jersey Office of Travel and Tourism, P.O. Box 820, Trenton, NJ 08625; (609) 777-0885 or (800) 847-4865; www.visitnj.org.

Spring Lake Chamber of Commerce, 302–304 Washington Ave., Spring Lake, NJ 07762; (732) 449-0577; www.springlake.org.

MID-ATLANTIC ESCAPE *Two*
Cape May—With or Without a Car
A SHORE THING / 2 NIGHTS

Off in a little world of its own, Cape May is sensationally situated on the southernmost tip of New Jersey, with the Atlantic Ocean on one side and the Delaware Bay on the other. It has been a popular beach resort since the days

- Victorian buildings
- Beach
- Boardwalk amusements
- Bicycling
- Bird-watching

of the American Revolution, and, in fact, is the oldest seashore resort in the country. Several U.S. presidents visited here, including Lincoln, Grant, Pierce, Buchanan, and Harrison, along with other names such as Horace Greeley and John Wanamaker.

Home to more than 600 Victorian buildings (many of which have been faithfully restored), Cape May is one of four U.S. seaports that have very successfully preserved their Victorian heritage. (Mendocino, California; Galveston, Texas; and Port Townsend, Washington, are the others.) In fact, the entire town has been proclaimed a National Historic Landmark and, for the most part, can be seen on foot.

The heart of town is the Washington Street Mall, which is a 3-block-long stretch closed to automobiles and lined with shops and restaurants. The real focus in Cape May, however, is the promenade, which runs along the Atlantic and its wide, sandy beach.

A long weekend here can be easily divided between a little sightseeing and some all-out relaxing. In between, there are several exceptionally good seafood restaurants to sample and many shops to browse through.

Keep in mind that some places close during the winter in Cape May. In spring, summer, and fall, many of the guest houses require

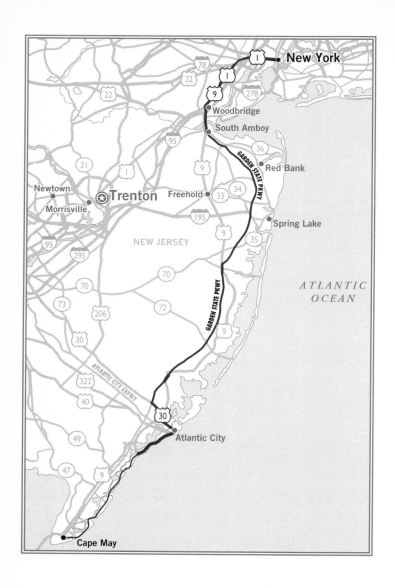

a two- to three-night minimum stay on weekends. If you want to avoid the crowds, go before Memorial Day or after Labor Day.

DAY 1 / MORNING

If you're going by car, follow the Garden State Parkway south as far as it will go (to exit 0). Then follow Lafayette right into Cape May. Expect to be in the car for about three hours, depending on traffic. From New York City, you can take a bus directly to Cape May. It's about a five to five-and-a-half hour trip and gets you right into the heart of town. For rates and schedules, go to www.njtransit.com.

When you arrive, first things first. If you have a car, your best bet is to park it somewhere, probably to stay put throughout your stay. Most of the hotels provide parking.

LUNCH　　　If you're in the mood for a light, healthy lunch, head over to **Gecko's** (Carpenter's Square Mall; 609-898-7750), where you'll find Southwestern cuisine.

AFTERNOON

After lunch, head over to the information booth on the corner of Ocean Street and the Mall to get in on a **Historic District Walking Tour.** The tour, which lasts about an hour and a half, is full of historical insights. Afterward, you may want to go back and explore on your own. You can do this on foot or by cruising around in a surrey bike (for rent, right behind Congress Hall).

DINNER　　　**Acamia,** 524 Washington St. Mall (609-884-6661) is a good dinner choice. You can sit outside and feast on a big salad or pasta dish and watch the people go by.

LODGING Congress Hall (251 Beach Ave.; 609-884-8421; www.con gresshall.com) is one of many wonderful places to call home while in Cape May. It has a lot of historic charm combined with new amenities—a comforting combination. In addition, it happens to be one of the most famous and most-photographed buildings in Cape May, painted a light yellow with white columns.

DAY 2 / MORNING

BREAKFAST You're going to wish you hadn't heard about **Uncle Bill's Pancake House** (609-884-7199). Located at Perry and Beach Avenues, though, it's hard to avoid if you're in Cape May. The problem with this place is that the pancakes are incredibly good—probably the best you've had in your life—and you'll inevitably eat way too many of them. There's always a crowd around breakfast time, but it moves fast.

After breakfast at Uncle Bill's, you're going to need a walk, so do as so many locals and visitors do: Walk the boardwalk. It's a tremendous way to start the day. After a while, head over to the **Emlen Physick Estate** (1048 Washington St.; 609-884-5404). This is a fully restored eighteen-room Victorian mansion designed by Frank Furness. If you have young children, find out when the kids' tour is. The estate is also headquarters for the **Mid-Atlantic Center for the Arts** (www.capemayac.org), which organizes several walking tours and trolley tours around town.

LUNCH The Carriage House Tearoom and Cafe (1048 Washington St.; 609-884-5111; www.capemaymac.org) is located right next to the Emlen Physick Estate's gift shop. Here you can make up for that calorie-rich breakfast by having light tea sandwiches. (The breads and sweet treats are mighty tempting, though.)

AFTERNOON

The afternoon is a good time to enjoy some beach time. Right offshore, you can actually see dolphins here. It's quite amazing.

DINNER **The Blue Pig Tavern** (251 Beach Ave.; 609-884-8422; www .congresshall.com) is always packed. Located in Congress Hall, it serves breakfast, lunch, and dinner. Among the dinner entrees are grilled portobello mushroom lasagna, buffalo and black bean chili, and Cajun-spiced shrimp skewers. You're sure to be happy.

DAY 3 / MORNING

BREAKFAST **The Mad Batter** (19 Jackson St.; 609-884-5970; www.mad batter.com) is a must-do in Cape May. Breakfast includes a choice of homemade fruit breads and muffins as well as substantial entrees.

Afterward, walk or bike out to **Cape May State Park** (follow Sunset Boulevard) for a beautiful walk through one of Cape May's best birding areas. There are 3 miles of trails and a boardwalk taking you over ponds and through wooded areas and marshlands. Then climb the 218 steps to the top of the **Cape May Lighthouse.**

Once you've had your fill of the ocean scenery, stop back in any shops you might have wanted to visit and start heading north out of town.

There's More . . . .

Bird-watching. Every fall, thousands of migratory birds (including everything from small songbirds to falcons and eagles) stop here on their way south. The best viewing areas are **Cape May State Park, the Cape May Migratory Bird Refuge,** and **Higbee's Beach.**

Fishing. There are several great fishing areas around Cape May, including the Second Avenue jetty and the World War II bunker by the lighthouse at **Cape May Point.**

Trolley tour. The **Cape May Point Trolley tour** is a 45-minute narrated trolley tour along Sunset Boulevard through Cape May Point. Many historical sites and points of interest are shown along the way, including the Cape May Lighthouse, St. Mary's by-the-Sea, and other historic houses. For more information, call (609) 884-5404 or visit www.capemaymac.org.

Special Events . . . .

APRIL
Tulip Festival, (609) 884-5508; www.capemaychamber.com.

APRIL AND NOVEMBER
Cape May Jazz Festival, (609) 884-7277; www.capemayjazz.org.

OCTOBER
Victorian Week, (609) 884-5508; www.capemaychamber.com.

DECEMBER
Christmas Candlelight Tour, (609) 884-5508; www.capemaychamber .com.

Other Recommended Restaurants and Lodgings . . . .

410 Bank Street, 410 Bank St.; (609) 884-2127. Some people drive to Cape May just to dine at 410 Bank St., and once there, you'll understand why. Every dish, every sauce is amazing here. Be sure to ask for a table on the porch.

The Ebbitt Room, 25 Jackson St.; (609) 884-5700; www.virginia hotel.com. Located in the Virginia Hotel, this restaurant has accumulated quite a few rave reviews. For the past several years, it has received awards for "Best Hotel Dining" and "Best Atmosphere," and well as "Best of the Best" by New Jersey Monthly readers.

The Virginia, 25 Jackson St.; (800) 732-4236; www.virginiahotel .com. There are just twenty-four rooms in this very elegant and intimate hotel that's a restored 1879 landmark building. It is on Jackson Street, in the heart of the historic district.

For More Information . . . .

Chamber of Commerce of Great Cape May, P.O. Box 556, Cape May, NJ 08204; (609) 884-5508; www.capemaychamber.com.

New Jersey Office of Travel and Tourism, P.O. Box 820, Trenton, NJ 08625; (609) 777-0885; www.visitnj.org.

INDEX